Berkshire Archaeological Committee
Publication no. 1

D1798666

THE MIDDLE THAMES VALLEY

An archaeological survey of the river gravels

Timothy Gates

1975

The cover is based on cropmarks at Ufton Nervet, and was designed by Mike Jarvis

© Berkshire Archaeological Committee 1975

Book no. 0 904989 00 3

Printed by TRUEXpress Oxford

CONTENTS

6

LIST OF ILLUSTRATIONS

ACKNOWLEDGEMENTS

I should like to thank the members of the Berkshire Archaeological Society's Air Photograph Group for supplying a number of photographs and maps, and for their help in the initial stages of plotting the cropmarks. Joan Bowman, Pat Crooke, Mike Dennis, Elspeth Grant, John Harvey and Joan Stevenson were particularly helpful.

I am grateful to the staff of the Berkshire County Planning Office for their cooperation and advice, particularly Mr Reo Muir, Mr George Weber and Mr Staniford of the minerals department.

The following kindly gave permission to reproduce photographs in their possession: Professor St Joseph *(plates 2, 4, 5, 7, 8, 9, 11, 12, 13, 14)*, The Air Photograph Unit of the National Monuments Record *(plate 6)*, Reading Museum *(plate 10)*, the Ashmolean Museum *(plate 1)*, and Henry Cheetham *(plate 3)*.

I am grateful to Tom Hassall for allowing the facilities of the Oxfordshire Archaeological Unit to be used in the preparation of the maps and figures, which were drawn by Robin Spey. I am particularly grateful to David Miles of the unit for his constant help and advice during the preparation of the survey.

The gazetteer was compiled with the help of information supplied by Reading Museum, the Field Department of the Oxford City and County Museum and the Buckinghamshire County Museum.

The maps are based on Ordnance Survey maps with the sanction of the Controller of H.M. Stationery Office; Crown Copyright Reserved.

The text was read by Richard Bradley, Hugh Haughton and Christopher Young and I am grateful for their comments.

This survey is printed with the aid of a grant from the Department of the Environment.

SUMMARY

The gravel terraces of the Thames and its tributaries are rich in ancient remains, which form a continuous record of occupation stretching back for over 5000 years. Modern development is rapidly destroying this record. This survey presents the archaeological evidence for settlement on the gravels as revealed by 30 years of aerial photography and fieldwork. Recommendations are put forward for a systematic programme of survey, excavation and selective preservation designed to reduce the destruction of important archaeological sites.

10

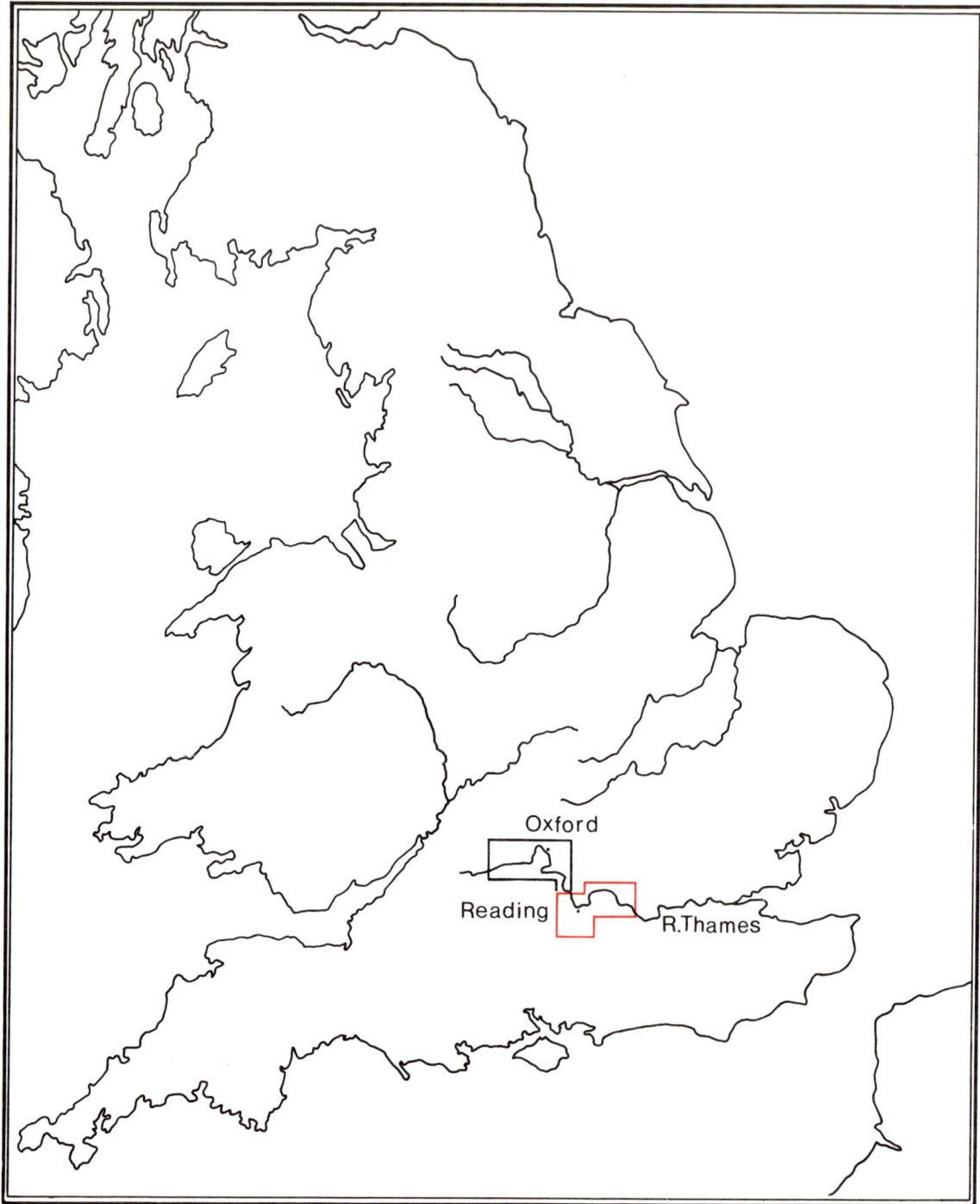

Fig. 1 Area covered by the Middle Thames survey shown in red and by the Upper Thames survey in black

1. INTRODUCTION

1.1   This survey presents the results of twenty five years of aerial survey work on the gravel terraces of the Middle Thames Valley. Cropmark complexes representing successive phases of settlement during the last 5000 years have been plotted on maps accompanied by descriptive notes and a commentary, thus making available a corpus of information that will be of interest to both archaeologists and non-specialists alike.

1.2   Modern development poses a threat to many of the cropmarked sites considered in this survey. Many more have been damaged or destroyed in the past without any record having been made of their presence. One of the principal aims of this survey is to bring areas with important remains to the attention of planning authorities and commercial developers, so that measures can be taken to preserve sites of outstanding regional or national importance, and to ensure adequate time and facilities for advance excavation where destruction is unavoidable.

1.3   This survey is restricted to a consideration of the gravel terraces of the river Thames between Goring and Wraysbury, a distance of approximately 40 miles. Also included are the gravels of the lower parts of the Kennet, Loddon and Blackwater valleys. Most of this area is contained within the new county of Berkshire apart from the terraces on the north side of the Thames which are divided between Oxfordshire and Buckinghamshire.

1.4   Sites on plateau gravels have for the most part been omitted although they are as important as those on the valley gravels and are similarly threatened by development. The thin sandy soil and scrub vegetation that are characteristic of many areas of plateau gravel inhibit cropmark development and prevent archaeological survey from the air.

1.5   When *A Matter of Time* was published by the Royal Commission on Historical Monuments in 1960 attention was drawn to the alarming rate at which archaeological sites on gravel were being destroyed in the course of development, particularly by gravel quarrying. Since then there have been disappointingly few regional surveys of the archaeological potential of gravel areas and the destruction has proceeded for the most part unchecked, in spite of some attentpts to deal with the problem on a local basis. For example in 1962 the Council for British Archaeology set up the Welland Valley Research Committee which for four years conducted a programme of rescue work on the gravels of the Welland valley. A similar temporary committee was set up by the CBA in 1968 to undertake a three-year survey and excavation programme in the Trent Valley. Although the final reports of both committees have yet to be published, interim reports confirm the archaeological richness of the gravels and underline the threat inherent in the rate of modern development. Some results of aerial survey work on the gravels of the Warwickshire Avon were published in 1964 (WEBSTER & HOBLEY 1964) but on the whole there has been no concerted attempt to make the results of aerial photography available to those in a position to take action over threatened sites. Against this background the publication of *The Upper Thames Valley: an archaeological survey of the river gravels* by the Oxfordshire Archaeological Unit in 1974 represents a major advance in the regional study of the problems raised by rescue archaeology. Cropmarked sites spread over a wide area were plotted in detail and presented together with a policy for the selective preservation and excavation of important sites, set against a background of current planning information. A similar format has deliberately been adopted in this survey so as to facilitate comparisons between the two areas.

1.6   The publication of this survey marks the second step in the formulation of a coherent regional policy for rescue archaeology in the Thames valley as a whole, and it is hoped that this will encourage a trend towards a broad approach to the problems of rescue archaeology elsewhere.

12

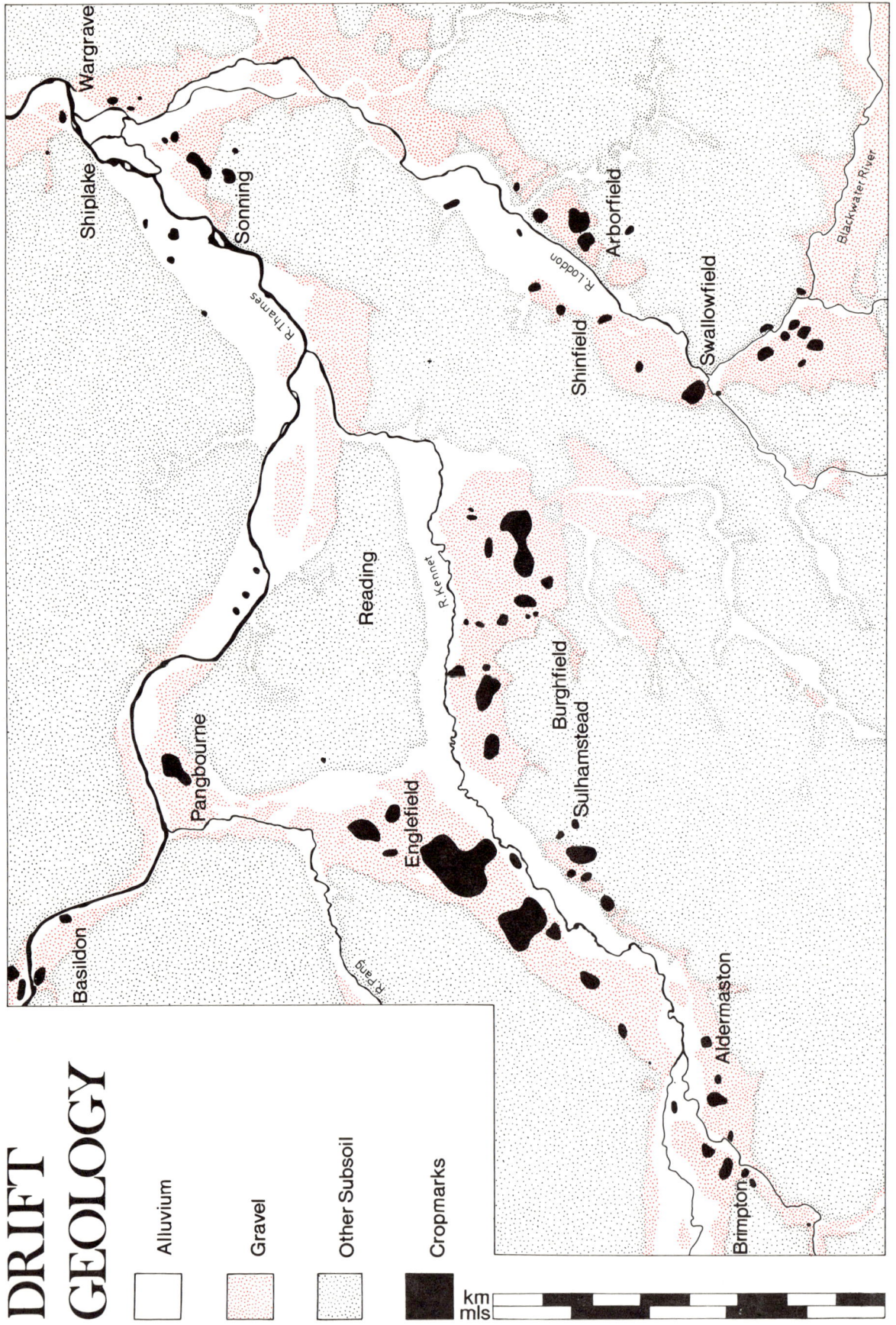

DRIFT GEOLOGY

Alluvium

Gravel

Other Subsoil

Cropmarks

km
mls

Basildon

Pangbourne

R. Pang

Reading

R. Kennet

Englefield

Sulhamstead

Burghfield

Aldermaston

Brimpton

Shiplake

Wargrave

Sonning

R. Thames

Shinfield

Arborfield

R. Loddon

Swallowfield

Blackwater River

Fig. 2a Drift geology Section 1 Thames Valley Goring-Shiplake, and lower Kennet, Loddon and Blackwater valleys

2. GRAVEL DEPOSITS

2.1   The gravels considered in this survey are bounded to the north by the chalk escarpment of the Chilterns and the Berkshire Downs. To the south lie the softer deposits of London clay which slope more gently away from the river than the more resistant chalk.

2.2   The Middle Thames gravels are predominantly composed of flint pebbles derived from the chalk and the overlying clay-with-flints. These have been deposited in a series of terraces by the Thames and its tributaries over the last 700,000 years. During this period northern Europe was subjected to a series of climatic deteriorations marked by glaciations interspersed with warmer periods when the ice sheets retreated. At the same time there were fluctuations in world sea level and the land masses were uplifted. As a result of these processes the river systems passed through alternate phases of downcutting and deposition which established the floodplain at successively lower levels. The eroded remains of these ancient floodplains can now be seen as terraces raised above the present river level. They form a sequence in descending order of age.

2.3   The terraced structure of these gravels is well developed in parts of the Middle Thames valley, particularly in the region of Slough where Professor Hare (1947) distinguished at least six main terraces above the modern floodplain. Each terrace is identified by a name corresponding to the locality in which it is most strongly marked and by its height above the modern floodplain. The generally accepted sequence is as follows: Taplow (30'), Lynch Hill (60'), Boyn Hill (110'), Winter Hill (190'), and Harefield (240'). A comparable sequence of terraces has been described in the valleys of the Kennet, Loddon and Blackwater rivers (THOMAS 1971). There are further high-level gravel sheets above the Harefield Terrace but they are thought to be of glacial origin and are strictly referred to as 'plateau gravels'.

2.4   The cropmarked sites considered in this survey are located mainly on the modern floodplain and the lower terraces. The upper terraces and high level gravel sheets are here collectively referred to as 'plateau gravels' in accordance with the boundary adopted by the Geological Survey on their 1″ survey maps. In general they produce cropmarks less readily than the lower gravels and are of a different character. Nevertheless there are sites on these gravels which are in need of survey, particularly in view of the high rate of gravel extraction on the south side of the Kennet valley between Burghfield and Greenham.

2.5   Whereas the distribution of the gravels in the Thames valley closely follows the course of the modern river, this is not the case in the area southwest of Reading where there is a discrepancy between the gravel distribution and the modern river system. The gravels north of Theale were deposited by the Kennet at a time when it joined the Thames at Pangbourne. At a later stage in the evolution of the river system the Loddon, or one of its tributaries, cut through the higher ground on which Reading now stands and formed the Coley gap. The Kennet was subsequently captured by the Loddon and diverted through this gap to join the Thames between Caversham and Sonning. The constriction imposed by the Coley gap caused the two rivers to meander over a wide area. This accounts for the wide floodplain southwest of Reading. At a still later stage the Loddon was itself captured by the Blackwater which it now joins at Swallowfield.

2.6   Compared with those of the Upper Thames basin the valley gravels of the Middle Thames are much less extensive, rarely exceeding a width of more than two miles except in the area to the east of Bray which is now largely covered by housing.

2.7   In general the valley gravels are capped by deposits of alluvium and brickearth to a depth of 1 to 2 metres. Weathering of these superficial deposits has formed light, free-draining soils that are easily worked and which have attracted farming communities since the introduction of agriculture into the British Isles in the fourth millenium BC. For many thousands of years before this the river valleys were periodically visited by nomadic bands of hunter-gatherers. Their abandoned stone tools were washed into the rivers and became incorporated into the gravel of the terraces. In the nineteenth and early twentieth centuries when gravel was dug and sieved by hand such palaeolithic tools were found in abundance in many pits in the region. Although these finds are beyond the scope of this book they are significant as evidence of early occupation and have been reviewed in a recent book by Wymer (1968).

14

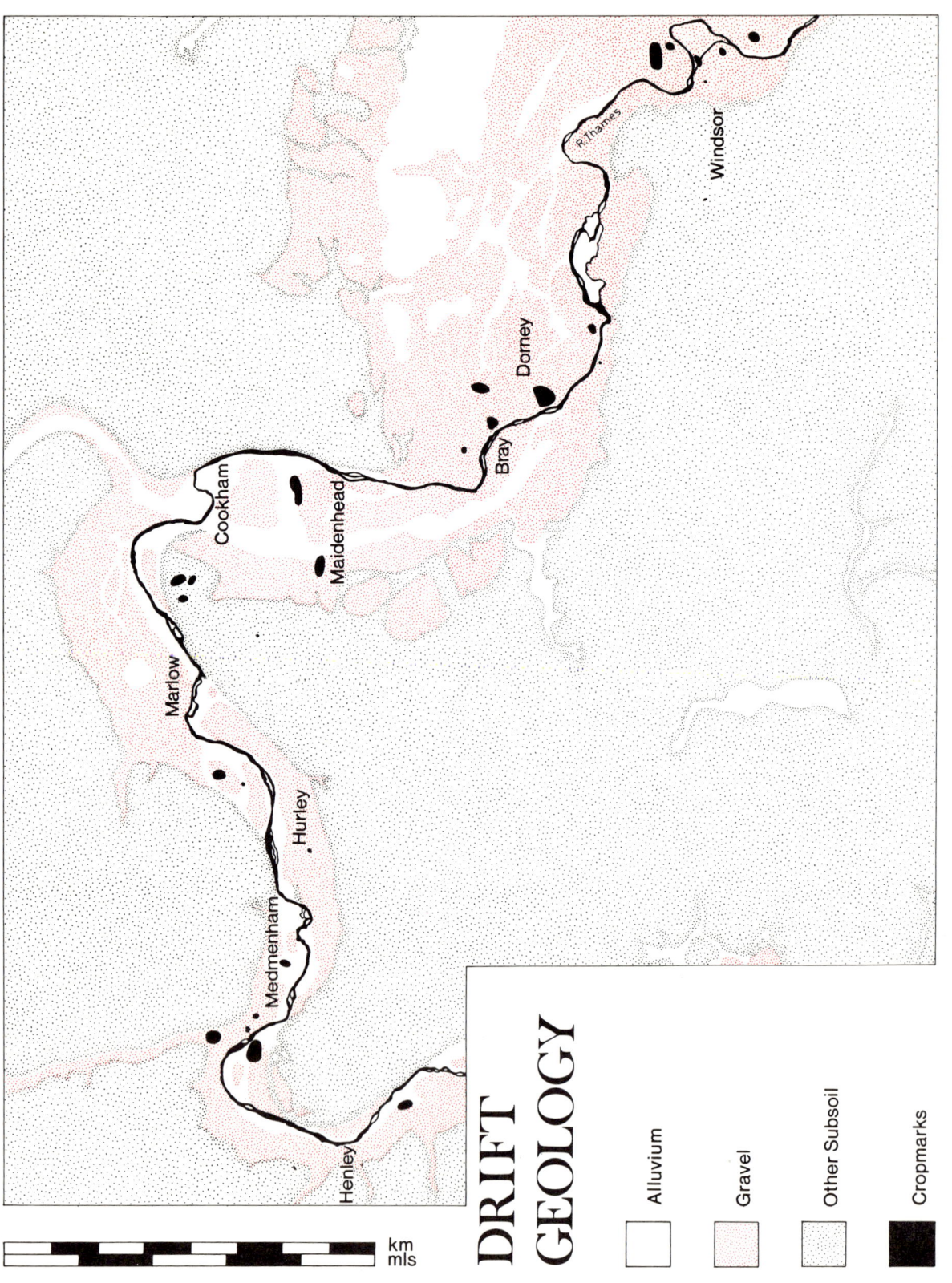

DRIFT
GEOLOGY

Alluvium

Gravel

Other Subsoil

Cropmarks

km
mls

Fig. 2b Drift geology Section 2 Thames Valley Shiplake-Wraysbury

Windsor

R.Thames

Dorney

Bray

Cookham

Maidenhead

Marlow

Hurley

Medmenham

Henley

3. FORMATION OF CROPMARKS

3.1   Cropmarks are lines or patches of different colour which can be seen in fields of ripening crops. They are produced as the result of differential growth and colouring of the crop in response to variations in the texture and moisture content of the underlying subsoil. The precise combination of circumstances that gives rise to these marks is not well understood but it is known to involve interactions between the drainage properties of the subsoil, the prevailing weather conditions and the nature of the crop itself. Excavation of cropmarked sites has repeatedly shown that they reflect underlying archæological and natural features of which the surface indications have usually been obliterated by ploughing.

3.2   Ditches and pits that were dug into the gravel in the distant past have long since silted up and no trace of them can be detected on the surface of modern fields. However where such features have become filled with fine silt they tend to retain moisture by capillary action more readily than does the surrounding coarser subsoil. As a result crop plants growing on top of them have improved access to water and mineral nutrients so that they grow more vigorously than their neighbours and turn a darker shade of green before ripening. The resulting patches or lines of taller, darker plants are termed 'positive cropmarks'. An example of this effect is illustrated in *Plate 1* which shows an early Iron Age ditch sectioned in the side of a gravel pit. The crop growing above the ditch is markedly darker and taller than that on either side where the soil is thinner. The reverse effect is produced by impervious features such as rubble foundations or solid floors. Where these lie close to the surface the crop is deprived of moisture and nutrients and its growth is inhibited, giving rise to a patch of pale, stunted plants described as a 'negative cropmark'. The development of both positive and negative cropmarks is illustrated diagrammatically in *Figure 3*.

   Although cropmarks can be distinguished at ground level or from the tops of buildings they are more readily interpreted and recorded when seen from the air.

3.3   Ancient earthworks that have been levelled by ploughing can in some instances still be distinguished by residual differences in soil colour and texture. For example the position of a ploughed-out barrow may be marked by a patch of light coloured soil representing the denuded remains of the mound, and ringed by a dark circle produced by the rich silt of the ditch filling. Such soilmarks are most commonly seen on chalklands where there is likely to be the greatest contrast in colour between the material used to construct a mound and the dark silt filling of ditches. One soil marked site has been included in the survey *(Map 5)*.

3.4   Crops vary considerably in their capacity to produce cropmarks, according to the length of their roots. Shallow rooted varieties like sugar beet or grass are usually insensitive to local variations in subsoil moisture and rarely exhibit cropmarks. Deep-rooted cereal crops, particularly wheat and barley, are much more sensitive and readily produce them. The subsoil itself exerts a strong influence on cropmark development. Free-draining subsoils like gravel greatly enhance the development of cropmarks because there is a marked contrast between the moisture content of the buried features and that of the surrounding undisturbed subsoil. On the other hand an impervious subsoil like clay inhibits their formation because there is little difference in the distribution of moisture between the subsoil and the filling of the man-made features.

3.5   The usefulness of aerial photography as a means of locating ancient settlements is necessarily limited to areas with a favourable subsoil which are given over to arable farming. These conditions are most often fulfilled in river valleys where the results of a consistent programme of aerial survey can be spectacular. A good example of this is provided by the work of Professor St Joseph on the distribution of round barrows in northeast Essex and east Suffolk. Up to 1959, 48 barrows of this type had been located in the area by ground fieldwork. After seven years of reconnaissance from the air this figure was increased to 250 and the distribution pattern completely changed (ST JOSEPH 1966). On the other hand no conclusions can be drawn from the absence of cropmarks in areas where local conditions are not conducive to their development. Even given promising local conditions, however, the vagaries of the weather and the changing pattern of land use introduce considerable uncertainty. It is therefore necessary to survey an area from the air over a number of years before a reliable impression of the true distribution of sites can be gained. In this respect the picture of changing settlement as revealed by aerial photography in the Upper Thames Valley is more com-

16

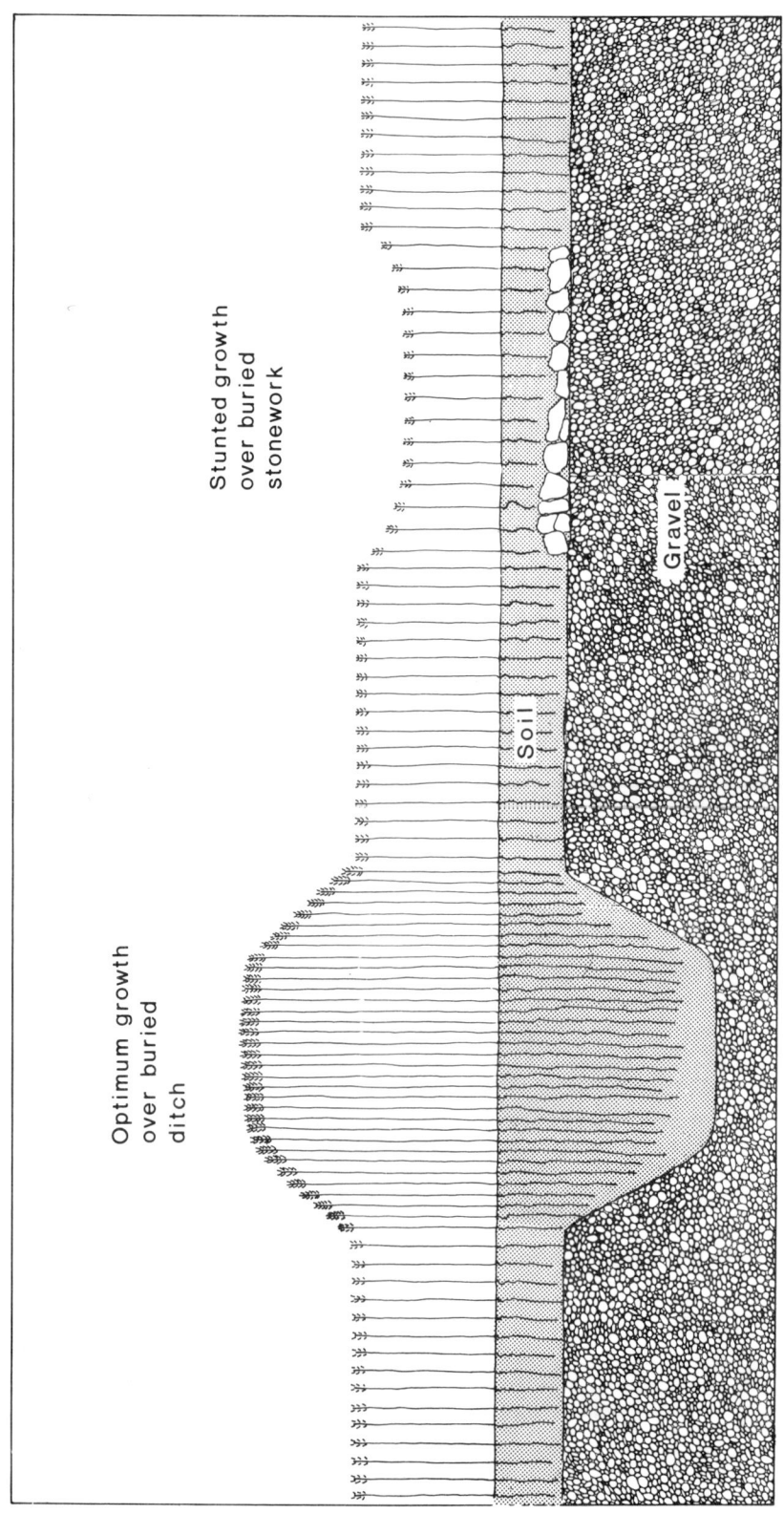

Optimum growth over buried ditch

Stunted growth over buried stonework

Soil

Gravel

Fig. 3 Diagram illustrating cropmark development

plete than in the Middle Thames where air survey has been conducted less intensively over a shorter period of time. The sites considered here must therefore be taken to represent only a proportion of the total number that actually exist. This is particularly true of the area to the east of Maidenhead where the flying restrictions imposed by Heathrow airport have limited air survey to only five flights.

3.6   A probable date and function can sometimes be assigned to particular types of cropmark by comparing them with undamaged monuments or excavation on similar sites elsewhere. Most circles probably indicate the sites of late Neolithic or Bronze Age barrows whose mounds have now been ploughed flat leaving only the infilled quarry ditch. Others may have been ceremonial or domestic enclosures surrounded by a circular bank and ditch. The majority of excavated examples can be shown to have been constructed between 2200BC and 1200BC. Smaller circles, in some cases associated with irregular enclosures, are usually taken to represent drainage gullies dug around huts. The huts themselves were in general not sufficiently substantial to have left traces visible from the air. Rectilinear enclosures associated with linear features and parallel lines generally indicate the presence of settlement sites or farms with their accompanying system of fields, stock enclosures and trackways. The smaller, more irregular examples may be of Iron Age date (800 BC-43AD) whilst the larger, rectangular ones are more likely to be Romano-British but can be earlier. Straight, parallel ditches running over long distances are interpreted as the side ditches of Roman roads. Scatters of dark spots mark the sites of pits, many of which were in use during the first millenium BC for storage purposes.

3.7   Not all cropmarked features are necessarily man-made. A variety of natural subsoil anomalies can also produce them. Silted up river meanders and frost cracks are sometimes indistinguishable from enclosures or field ditches (WILLIAMS 1973). Natural pockets of clay occuring near the surface of the gravel may look very like pits. It is probable that at least a few of these features have been plotted on the maps in this survey as they can be very difficult to distinguish from archaeological cropmarks.

———————————— O ————————————

4. HISTORY

Cropmarks and Aerial Photography

4.1   Cropmark photography in the Middle Thames valley has lagged 20 years behind that in the Upper Thames. None of the early flyers, such as Crawford, Allen or Riley, took any photographs of sites below Goring and the area remained unsurveyed from the air until well after the second world war.

4.2   The first air photographs of cropmarks on the Middle Thames gravels were taken by Professor St Joseph in 1948, since when he has continued surveying the region and to date has made more than 60 individual flights over the gravels. Many of the sites documented in this survey were first photographed by him. The high quality of St Joseph's oblique photographs and the extent of his air coverage make the Cambridge University collection of photographs the most important source of cropmark information for the Middle Thames.

4.3   The second major source of air photographs is the collection assembled by the Air Photograph Unit of the National Monuments Record under the direction of John Hampton. Between 1965 and 1972 the Unit has made about 20 flights over the gravels re-photographing sites discovered by St Joseph and locating many new ones.

4.4   Between 1959 and 1964 several short flights from local aerodromes were sponsored by regional organisations, including the Reading University Museum of Rural Life, Reading University Department of History, the Berkshire Archaeological Society, the Berkshire Chronicle and Reading Museum, for the specific purpose of photographing cropmarks. As a result of these flights a number of sites became known locally for the first time even though they had been recorded previously during surveys conducted from Cambridge or London. Several excavations were organised in the early 1960s to test the results of these local flights.

More recently, regular flights have been undertaken by local archaeologists, notably Dick and Jill Greenaway, and by a number of amateur enthusiasts. Unless the resources of the Air Photograph Unit of the National Monuments Record and the Cambridge Committee for Aerial Photography are substantially increased the task of comprehensive annual air survey will necessarily have to be undertaken by organisations from within the region itself.

Plotting and Synthesis of Aerial Photographs

4.5 To date less than 1% of the total number of aerial photographs of sites on the Middle Thames gravels has been published and there are no published distribution maps of cropmarked areas or of individual types of site. As a result there has been a general lack of awareness at both local and national levels of the extent of ancient settlement on the gravels. Consequently a number of sites have either been totally destroyed or seriously damaged in the course of development, with little or no attempt at prior recording or excavation. Even the publication of *A Matter of Time* in 1960, which specifically drew attention to the threat to archaeological sites inherent in development on gravels, provoked no attempt to assess the scale of the problem in the Middle Thames area until the present survey was commissioned by the Department of the Environment in 1974.

4.6 The first systematic attempt to plot cropmarks in the region began in 1973 when members of the Berkshire Archaeological Society, under the direction of Richard Bradley, obtained a grant from the Carnegie fund (United Kingdom) with which to buy maps and photographs. A number of valuable plots at both 6″ and 25″ to the mile were finished and are now kept in Reading Museum.

Excavation

4.7 Fewer than ten excavations, for either research or rescue purposes, have been conducted on gravel sites in the Middle Thames valley and consequently little is known about changing patterns of settlement or land use in the area. This is in contrast to the Upper Thames, where there were almost one hundred and eighty excavations on gravel during the period 1930-70, of which the great majority were rescue operations. Even there the piecemeal nature of the excavations and the lack of published information have provided only a very incomplete and fragmented picture of the changing archaeological landscape.

4.8 Before 1960 there had been only two informative excavations on gravel in the middle Thames area; one was a Roman villa excavated in 1912 at Hambleden in Buckinghamshire (COCKS 1921) and the other an extensive Saxon settlement thought to be connected with Edward the Confessor's palace at Old Windsor, Berkshire; (though a final report has never been published, see WILSON & HURST 1958 for a preliminary note). Otherwise knowledge of settlement on the gravels was restricted to stray finds and unstratified material recovered from gravel pits or encountered during railway construction in the nineteenth century (eg PIGGOTT 1936; PIGGOTT & SEABY 1937; SMITH 1840; & *Arch. Journ.* XV, 1858, p. 287).

4.9 Four research excavations conducted in the early 1960s were planned as a direct result of cropmarks observed on flights sponsored by local bodies during the exceptionally dry summer of 1959 (*4.4*). A subrectangular enclosure adjacent to the cursus at Sonning proved to be of Neolithic date and is thought to have had a ceremonial function (SLADE 1964). A complex of enclosures and trackways at Ufton Nervet were shown to date from the late Iron Age and early Roman periods, and probably represent a farmstead which was rebuilt on a more regular plan after the Roman invasion (*BAJ* 1962; *JRS* 1964; & MANNING *BAJ* — in press). One of a group of four conjoined ring-ditches at Englefield was excavated and Neolithic pottery found in the fill of the ditch. A smaller ring-ditch at Sonning was sectional but could not be dated. Only preliminary notes on these last two excavations have so far been published (*BAJ* 1960, p. 63; *BAJ* 1964, p. 100). Since 1964 there have also been several small scale rescue excavations in gravel pits and along the route of the M4, which have been reported in the 'Notes from Reading Museum' in the *BAJ*.

Organisation

4.10 The haphazard and often inadequate response to the destruction of archaeological sites on the Middle

Thames gravels in the past has been largely due to a lack of awareness of the significance of cropmarks and their distribution in the region. Last-minute salvage excavations were usually only attempted as hitherto unknown sites were revealed and almost simultaneously destroyed in the course of gravel digging or road construction. As recently as 1970 large sites which had previously been recorded by aerial photography were destroyed or damaged without record when the M4 was built (see *Plates 7 & 8*) because no local person knew of the existence of the relevant aerial photographs. Until 1974 only one rescue excavation on gravel had been planned in advance and that was a direct result of the publication of a single air photograph in *A Matter of Time* (RCHM 1960; Plate 6a). Of necessity excavations were conducted on an *ad hoc* basis without reference to any theoretical framework from which to derive a scale of priorities. In consequence much of the information that was receovered is now of limited value whilst elsewhere important sites were destroyed without examination. The lack of any formal body responsible for recording sites in advance of destruction meant that this task fell to already overworked local institutions or individuals with different priorities and strictly limited resources. At various times these have included Reading Museum, Reading University, the Berkshire Archaeological Society and other local societies and individuals. To say that the past response to the destruction of gravel sites has been inadequate is to acknowledge the difficult circumstances which militated against the formulation of a coherent regional strategy for rescue archaeology and in no way implies criticism of those who, in many cases voluntarily, made efforts to tackle the problem.

4.11   As a result of increasing awareness of the need to consider the problem of rescue archaeology on a regional basis, the Berkshire Archaeological Committee was formed in late 1973 to set up an organisation to carry out rescue work on a systematic basis in the new county of Berkshire. The Committee represents a broad range of opinion and includes representatives of local government, local institutions and societies, and the Department of the Environment. In March 1974 it appointed a field officer to undertake a survey of the gravels and to conduct rescue excavations on threatened sites. The following June two additional field officers were appointed to deal respectively with threats connected with urban developments and projected road schemes. In April 1975 responsibility for the coordination of all rescue work in Berkshire was assumed by the newly formed Berkshire Archaeological Unit.

———————— O ————————

5. INTRODUCTION TO THE GAZETTEER

5.1   As previously emphasised *(3.5)* the distribution of the cropmarks plotted here represents the state of our present knowledge. As aerial survey of the gravels progresses further cropmark complexes will undoubtedly be found in areas that now appear blank on the maps.

5.2   The gazetteer is divided into two sections:
    Section 1:   The Thames gravels from Goring to Shiplake together with the gravels in the lower parts of the Kennet, Loddon and Blackwater river valleys.
    Section 2:   The Thames gravels from Shiplake to Wraysbury.

5.3   All the maps are drawn to coincide with National Grid kilometre squares. The cropmarks were originally drawn from oblique photographs at a scale of 1:10560 (6″ to the mile). As a result of plotting at this small scale the marks are of limited accuracy and lacking in fine detail, though in most cases they are within 15 metres of their true position. The maps are intended to convey an impression of the character and distribution of the cropmarks rather than their precise location. The sites of major excavations have been indicated by a star and known sites which do not appear as cropmarks by a spot.

5.4   The cropmarks on each map are described in sequence by kilometre square and no attempt has been made to define individual sites or to distinguish sites of different periods. After each kilometre square number the relevant OS 6″ map number is given followed by a 6-figure map reference and the parish name.

CROPMARKS

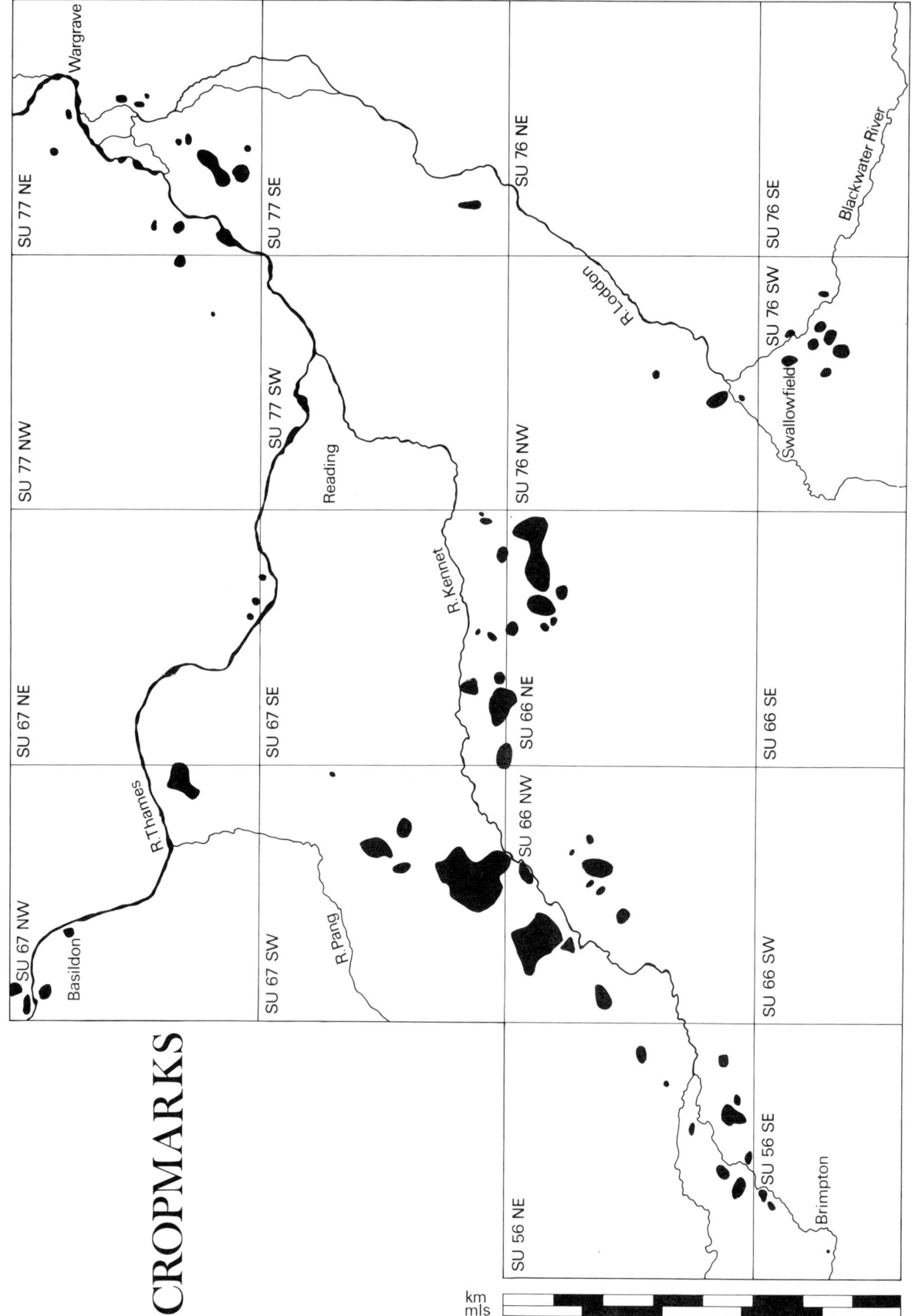

Fig. 4 Distribution of cropmarks in Section 1 Thames Valley Goring-Shiplake, and lower Kennet, Loddon and Blackwater valleys

21

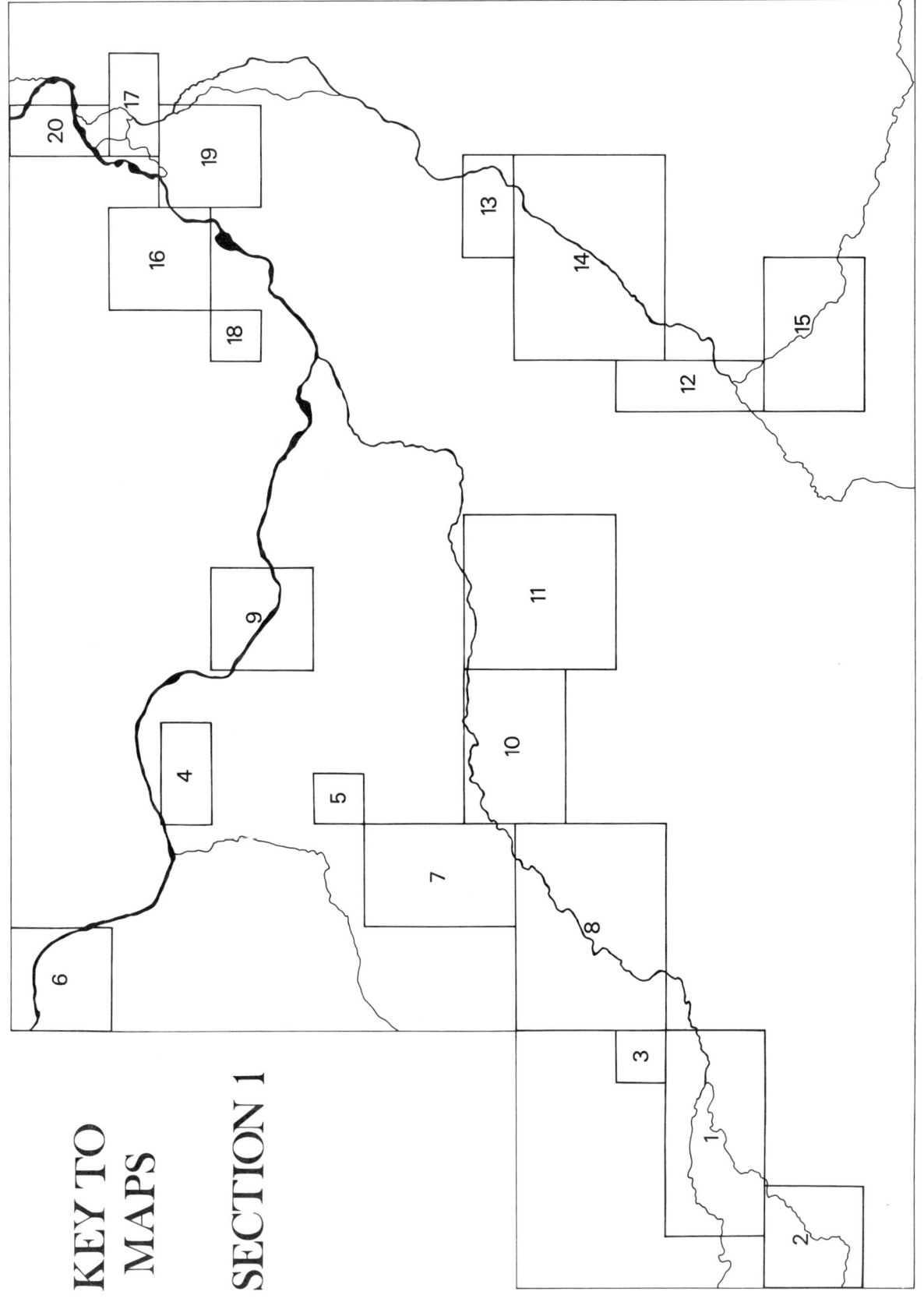

KEY TO
MAPS

SECTION 1

Fig. 5 Key to cropmarks maps in Section 1

5.5   As far as possible the cropmarks have been described in purely geometrical terms (eg. circle, rectangular enclosure) so as to avoid assumptions about date and function. The authors of the Upper Thames gravels survey have been followed in the use of the term 'block mark' to describe solid, oblong rectangular marks which are thought to represent small gravel quarries or marl pits and are often associated with evidence of medieval agriculture.

5.6   The description of the features in each square is followed by a list of abbreviations which indicate the numbers of the negatives of the prints that were used to plot the features, and the source from which they were obtained. The following abbreviations are used:

ST JOSEPH:	Committee for Aerial Photography, University of Cambridge, 11 West Road, Cambridge. Photographs taken by Professor J.K.S. St Joseph.
NMR:	Air Photograph Unit, National Monuments Record, 23 Savile Row, London W1X 1AB. Photographs taken by John Hampton.
RM:	Reading Museum, PO Box 17, Town Hall, Reading. Photographs from a variety of sources.
BAU:	Berkshire Archaeological Unit.

5.7   The year in which a particular photograph was taken is indicated immediately after the abbreviation of the source. Thus ST JOSEPH 57 VF 84 indicates that the photograph was taken by St Joseph in 1957 and that the number of the negative is VF 84.

5.8   Where there is additional information concerning a feature either in a publication or in Ordnance Survey records then this has been summarised and an appropriate reference given after each entry. For sites in Oxfordshire, primary record numbers are quoted (PRN). They refer to the record number allocated to the site in the Sites and Monuments Record, Oxford City and County Museum, Woodstock.

5.9   The following abbreviations are used: Neo (Neolithic), BA (Bronze Age), IA (Iron Age), RB (Romano-British) and DMV (Deserted Medieval Village). The abbreviation *BAJ* is a reference to the 'Notes from Reading Museum' published in volumes of the Berkshire Archaeological Journal and is followed by an appropriate volume and page number.

5.10   The route of the M4 motorway is not shown on maps 10, 11 and 14 because the relevant OS 6″ maps have not yet been revised to include it. Where motorway developments affect cropmarked sites this is recorded in the gazetteer.

———————————— O ————————————

SECTION 1. CROPMARKS IN THE THAMES VALLEY
BETWEEN GORING AND SHIPLAKE, AND IN THE LOWER KENNET, LODDON, AND BLACKWATER VALLEYS

Map 1

5665 SU 56 NE Area centred SU 568653
BRIMPTON
Parallel side-ditches of Roman road leading from Silchester (Calleva Atrebatum), 4½ miles to SE, to Cirencester. To W irregular linear features.
ST JOSEPH 69 AYH 28, 30.
NMR 70 SU 5764/1/178-180.

5765 SU 56 NE Area centred SU 573651
WASING
Roman road (see 5665 above). Single circle. Irregular enclosure N of Roman road. Ridge and furrow.
ST JOSEPH 69 AYH 30.
NMR 70 SU 5764/1/181.

5765 SU 56 NE Area centred SU 572656
BRIMPTON
3 superimposed rectangular enclosures. Linear features to NE and SW.
ST JOSEPH 61 ADN 50-51; 69 AYH 27, 29.
Site totally destroyed by gravel quarrying without investigation.

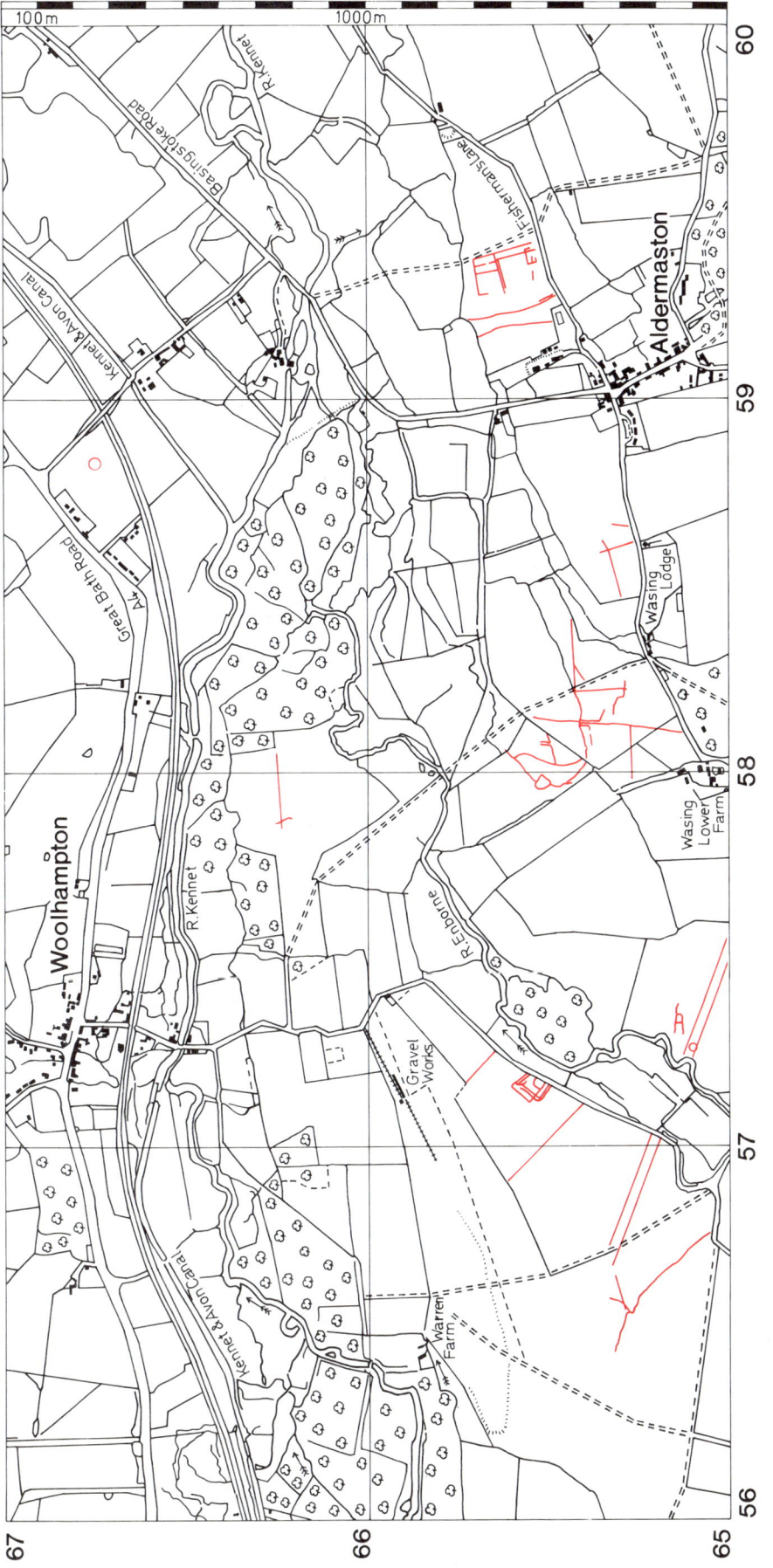

Map 1. Cropmarks around Aldermaston and Woolhampton

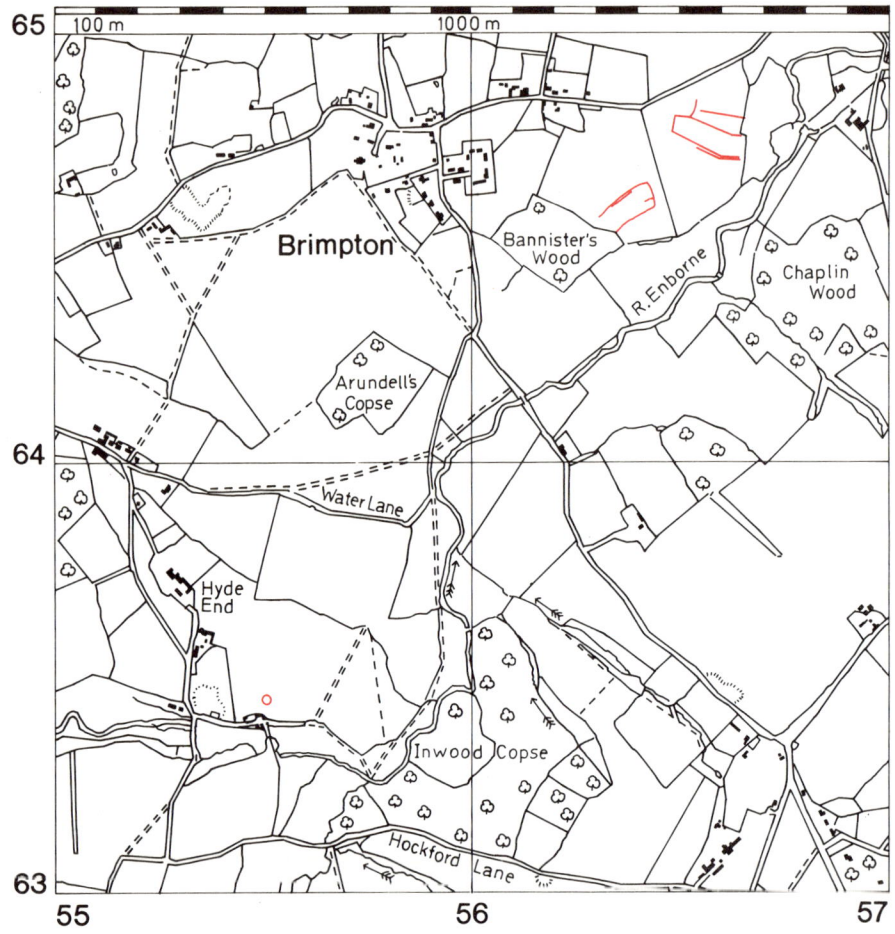

Map 2. Cropmarks around Brimpton

(Map 1 continued)

5766 5866 SU 56 NE Area centred SU 579662 WOOLHAMPTON
Intersecting linear features.
NMR 70 SU 5865/2/171.

5765 5865 SU 56 NE Area centred SU 581654 WASING and ALDERMASTON
Complex linear and curvilinear features with short parallel lines in two places. Irregular enclosure at 579655. Intersecting linear features to E at 586653.
ST JOSEPH 69 AYH 34.
NMR 70 SU 5765/1; SU 5865/1/157-158, 161; /2/165, 167-168; SU 5965/2/156.

5866 SU 56 NE Area centred SU 588667 WOOLHAMPTON
Single circle.
NMR 70 SU 5866/1/172-174; 70 SU 5866/2.

5965 SU 56 NE Area centred SU 593656 ALDERMASTON
Rectangular enclosure with internal divisions, including one with entrance. Second rectangular enclosure to S connected to first by parallel lines. Curvilinear features to W.
ST JOSEPH 69 AYH 35-36.
NMR 70 SU 5965/2/151-153.

Map 2

5463 SU 56 SW Area centred SU 549636 BRIMPTON
Trackway and linear features. Not plotted.
NMR 70 SU 5563/1/182, 185.

5563 SU 56 SE Area centred SU 555635 BRIMPTON
Single circle.
NMR 70 SU 5563/1/182, 185.

5664 SU 56 SE Area centred SU 565647 BRIMPTON
Irregular elongated enclosure with double ditches in part and adjacent linear features on N side. Second irregular enclosure to SW at 563646.
ST JOSEPH 69 AYH 31-33.
Site of House of the Knights Hospitaller at Shalford Farm.

Map 3

5967 SU 56 NE Area centred SU 595673 BEENHAM
Rectangular enclosure. Incomplete circle. Pits and linear features.
ST JOSEPH 60 ABX 52.

Map 3. Cropmarks south of Beenham

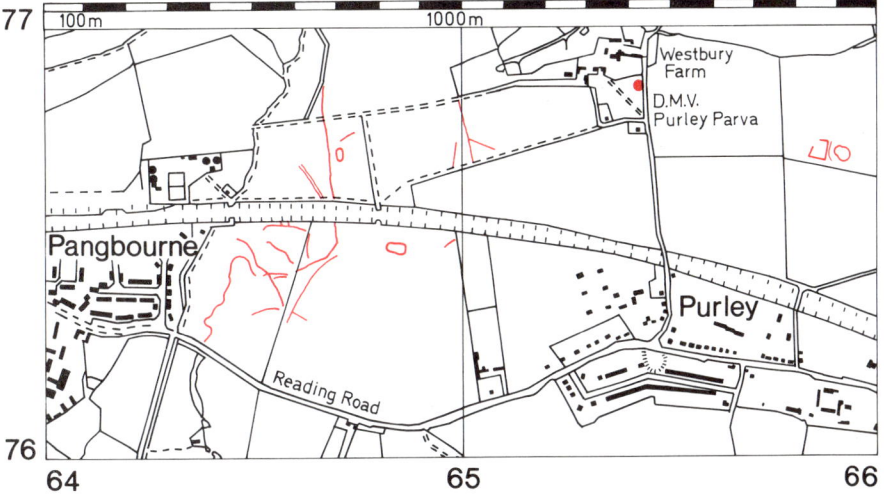

Map 4. Cropmarks between Pangbourne and Purley

Map 4

6476 SU 67 NW Area centred SU 646764
PURLEY
Curvilinear features (abandoned river
meanders ?). Linear features, some of
which may be pipelines or field drains. To
E at 648765 trapezoidal enclosure with
rounded ends (c.45m long) and short
linear feature. To N at 647767 oval enclosure (c.30m long), linear features and
trackway. To NE at 650767 isolated
linear features (field drains?).
NMR 70 SU 6476/1,2,5,/7/150, 153.

6576 SU 67 NE Area centred SU 659767
PURLEY
2 conjoined circles, rectangular enclosure
and curvilinear feature.
ST JOSEPH 66 AOJ 71.

Map 5

6473 SU 67 SW Area centred SU 639735
SULHAM
Single circle and small open sided enclo-
sure to E. Soil mark.
ST JOSEPH 72 BHZ 11-12.

Map 6

6079 SU 67 NW Area centred SU
607793
BASILDON
Rectangular enclosures, linear features and
pits near to the sites of 2 Roman buildings.
To W incomplete circle, parallel lines and
curvilinear feature.
ST JOSEPH 62 AFT 45; 70 BCH 63.
NMR 70 SU 6079/2/144, 146.

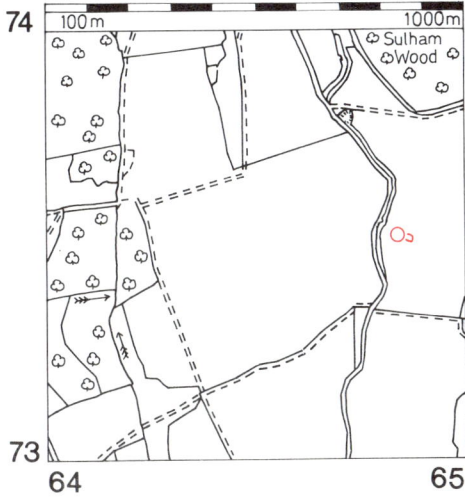

Map 5. Soilmarks south of Sulham

Roman building at 60747933 destroyed during railway construction in 1839 (*Archaeologia* 1840, *40*, p.447-450). Second Roman building at 605792 damaged by road widening in 1967.

6079 SU 67 NW Area centred SU 604797
GORING
Group of 8 circles, including 2 double concentric circles, and 4 incomplete ones. Parallel lines to W (trackway ?).
ST JOSEPH 59 YO 47; 62 AFT 45; 66 AOJ 75; 70 BCH 62-63.
NMR 70 SU 6079/2/141, 144.

6079 SU 67 NW & 6080 SU 68 SW Area centred SU 606799
GORING
4 circles. Pair of slightly divergent lines, possibly a cursus. Incomplete rectangular enclosure with internal pits at one end of ?cursus. To SE small incomplete rectangular enclosure and linear features.
ST JOSEPH 59 YO 45, 47; 70 BCH 60, 62.
PRN 1931.

6178 SU 67 NW Area centred SU 617788
BASILDON *Pl. 2*
Incomplete double rectangular enclosure with parallel linear feature along S side. Second enclosure or linear feature cuts across N side at right angles.
ST JOSEPH 61 ADN 15; 59 YO 40, 42.
Site described by St. Joseph in *Antiquity* 1967, *41*, p. 312 & pl.XLIV.

Map 7

6270 SU 67 SW Area centred SU 624702
SULHAMSTEAD *Pl. 3*
Linear group of 4 contiguous circles crossed by linear feature. Parallel linear feature to NW.
ST JOSEPH 59 YD 44; 61 ADN 35.
NMR 70 6270/2/426.
RM 62 CM 59-61.
Excavation of the small NE circle in 1963 by Wymer and Ashbee showed it to be 50 feet in diameter and truncated by its westerly neighbour. The ditch contained fragments of Windmill Hill, Mortlake, Rinyo-Clacton, and Beaker pottery. (*BAJ* 1964, *61*, p.100).

6270 SU 67 SW Area centred SU 624706
SULHAMSTEAD and ENGLEFIELD
5 rectangular and subrectangular enclosures with scattered pits and 2 small circles. Isolated linear feature to W at 622706. Linear group of 2 complete and 2 incomplete circles at 624706 with adjacent linear feature.
ST JOSEPH 61 ADN 32; 62 SFV 36; 69 AYH 14-15, 17; 70 BCH 66.
NMR 70 SU 6270/1/422-423, 425,/5/456, 458, 460, 462.

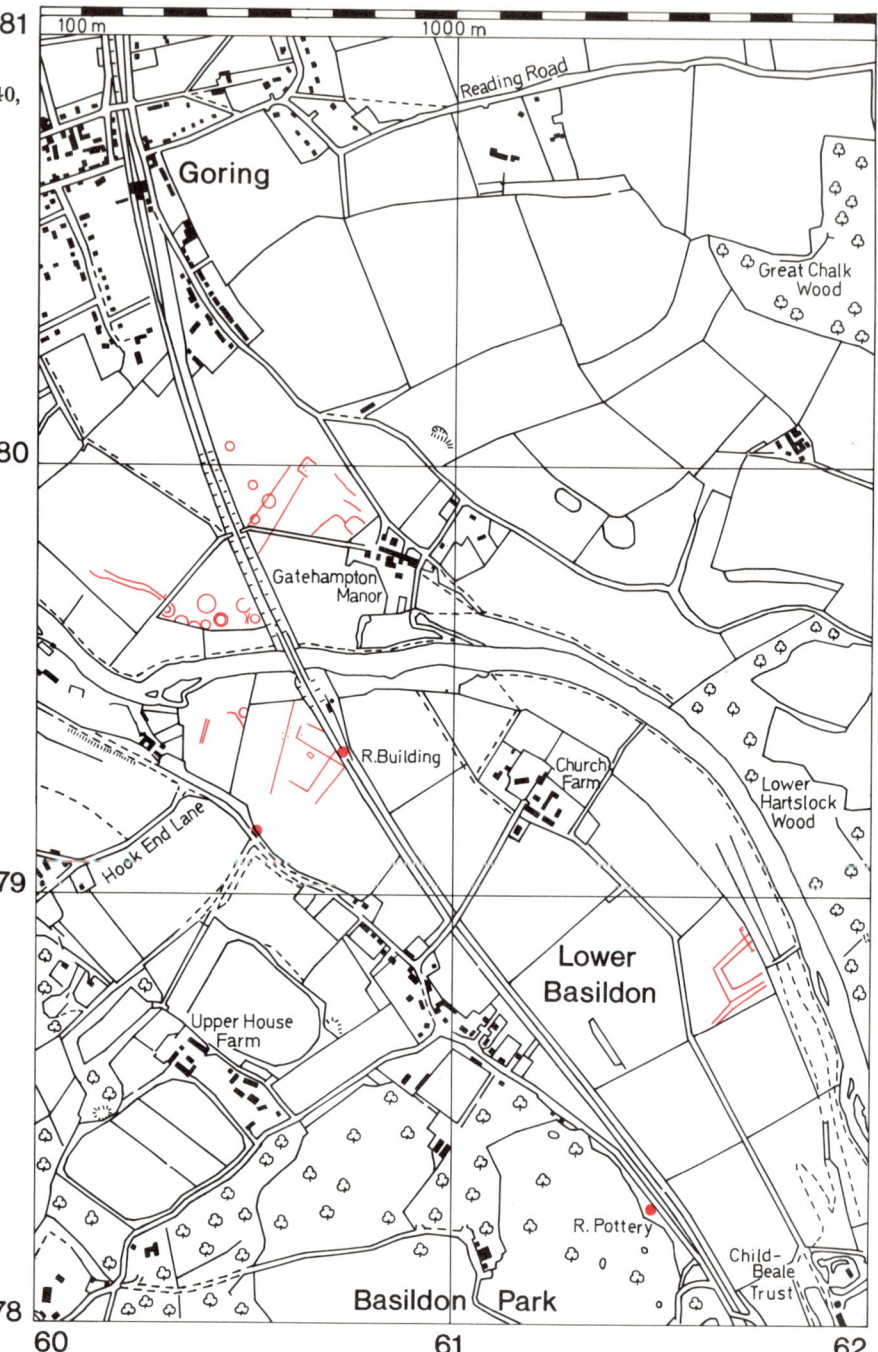

Map 6. Cropmarks around Goring and Basildon

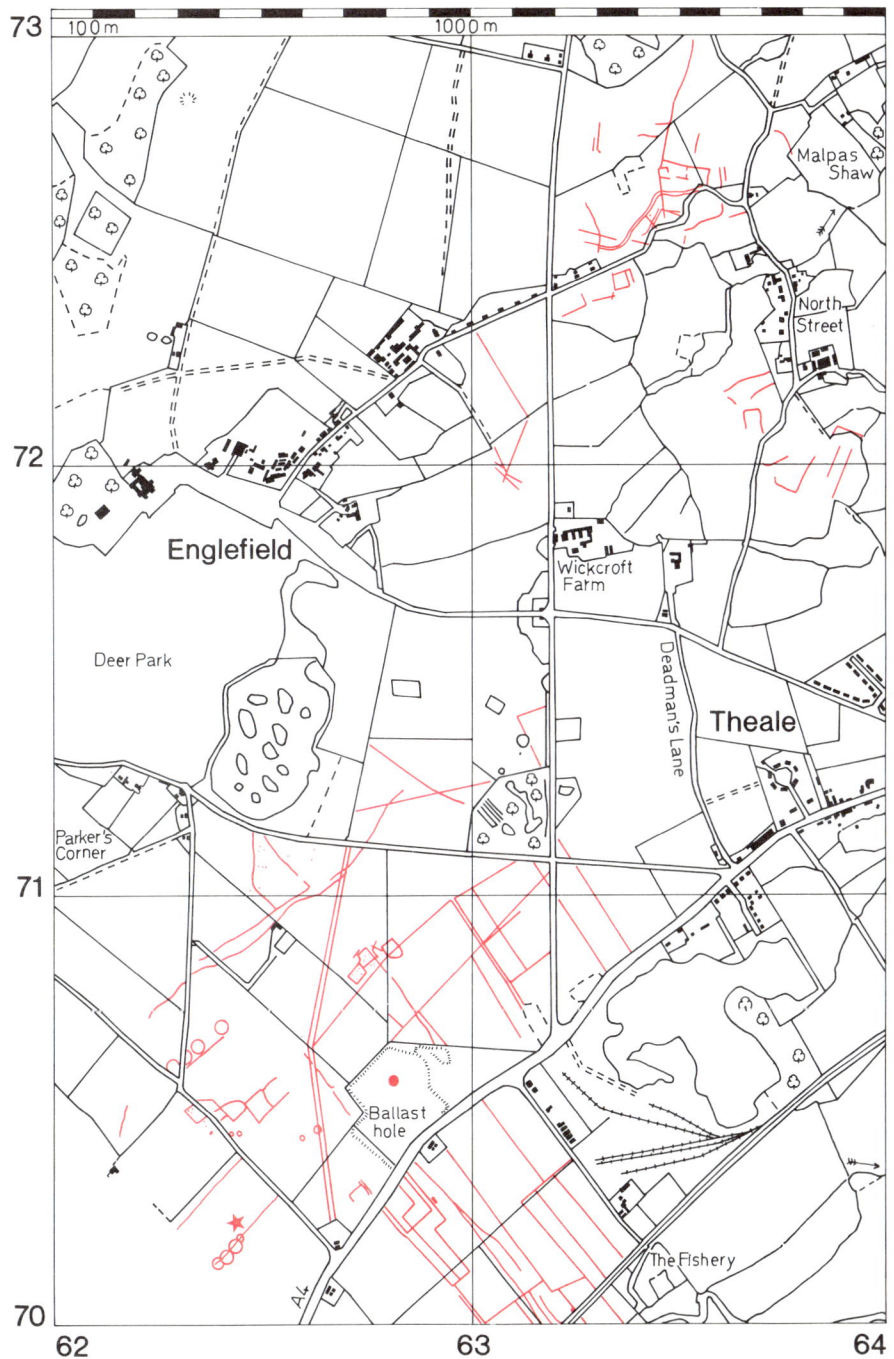

Map 7. Cropmarks around Englefield

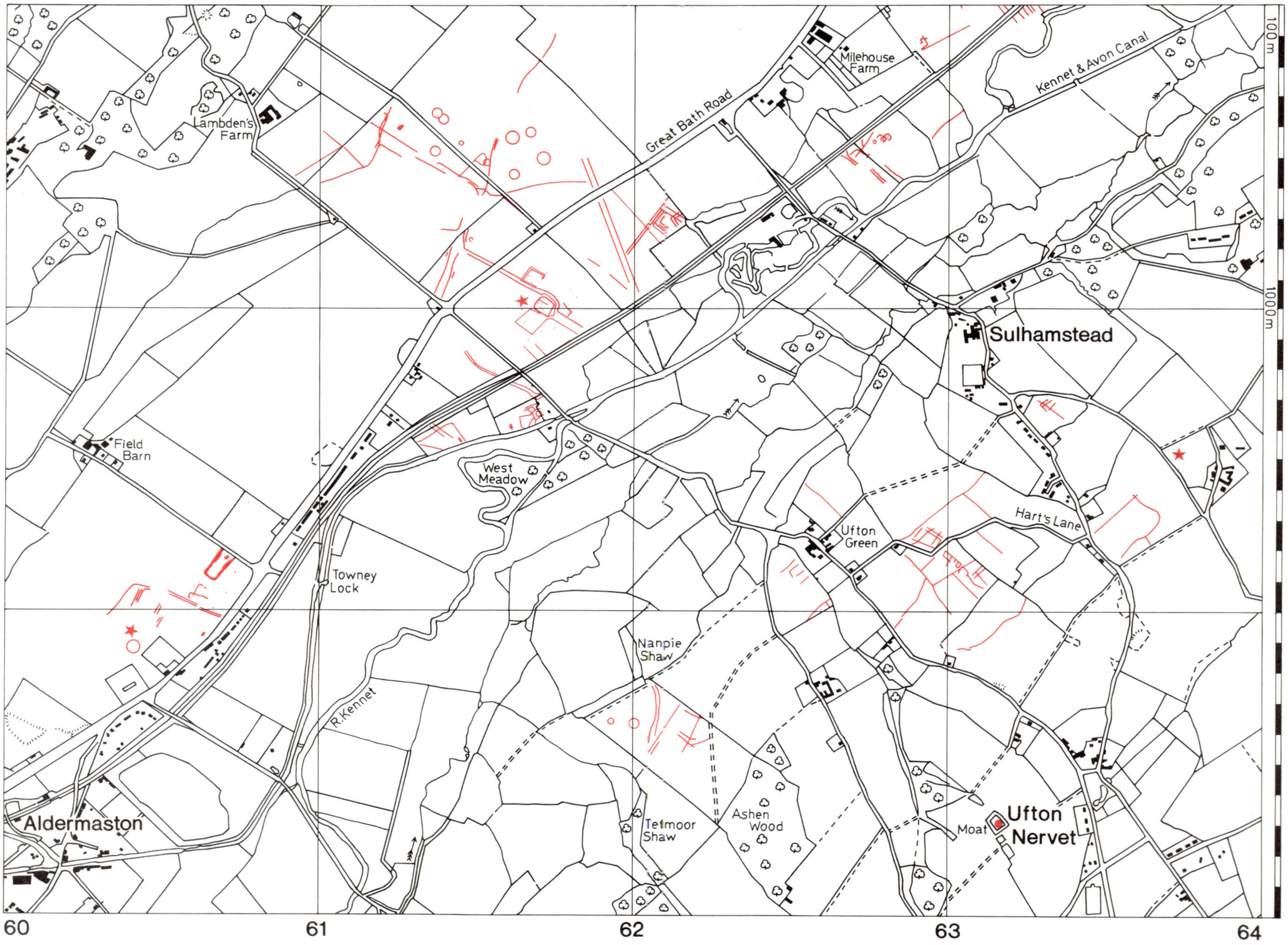

100 m   1000 m

64

Kennet & Avon Canal

Sulhamstead

Hart's Lane

Ufton Nervet

Moat

Ufton Green

Milehouse Farm

Great Bath Road

Ashen Wood

Nanpie Shaw

Tetmoor Shaw

63

62

West Meadow

Towney Lock

R. Kennet

Lambden's Farm

Field Barn

Aldermaston

61

60

70   69   68   67

Map 8   Cropmarks around Ufton Nervet and Sulhamstead

6270 SU 67 SW Area centred SU 626703
ENGLEFIELD
Straight road running SSE-NNW and bend-
ing at 626707 to run SSW-NNE. Small
circle at 627704 with second small circle to
W. Linear feature intersected by road.
ST JOSEPH 59 YD 47, 50; 62 AFV 36; 69
AYH 14; 70 BCH 66, 68.
NMR 70 SU 6270/1/423, 425,/3,/4/429,/5/
456, 458, 460, 462,/6/123, 125; 70 SU
6370/4/443.
The road ditches are said to be those of a
road shown on an Ordnance Survey 2"
map of 1809.

6270 SU 67 SW Area centred SU 627702
ENGLEFIELD
Rectangular enclosure with parallel lines
along E side.   NMR 70 SU 6270/1/425,
/3,/4/431,433,/5/460,462.

6270 SU 67 SW Area centred SU 628709
ENGLEFIELD and THEALE
3 subrectangular enclosures with linear
features and scattered pits.
ST JOSEPH 59 YD 47, 50-51, 57; 61 ADN
32; 70 BCH 66, 68-69.
NMR 70 SU 6270/5/456, 458, 460,/6/123,
125; 70 SU 6370/4/443, 445.

6270 6271 SU 67 SW Area centred SU
625710   ENGLEFIELD
Large irregular enclosure with entrance on
NE side. Irregular lines to SW. Scattered
pits.
ST JOSEPH 59 YD 47, 50-51; 70 BCH 68.
NMR 70 SU 6270/1/422,/5/456,458; 71
SU 6270/7/127.

6271 SU 67 SW Area centred SU 629712
ENGLEFIELD
Intersecting linear features.
NMR 70 SU 6370/4/441, 443.

6270 6370 SU 67 SW Area centred SU
631702
ENGLEFIELD and THEALE
Extensive complex of elongated rectangular enclosures. Block marks at 629702
and 632700.
NMR 70 SU 6270/4/431, 433, 435, /5/465,
469, 471; 70 SU 6370/4/450, 453, 455.

6270 6370 6271 6371 SU 67 SW Area
centred SU 630709
THEALE
Extensive complex of large rectangular
enclosures similar to those described in
6270 and 6370 above, but divided by
trackway.
ST JOSEPH 59 YD 52, 56; 64 AJH 92;
70 BCH 66, 68-69.
NMR 70 SU 6370/2, /3, /4/441, 443, 445,
447, 448.
Gravel quarrying at the 'Ballast Hole' in the
1930s brought to light an important series
of pottery ranging from Iron Age to Saxon
date (PIGGOTT 1936 & 1938).

6370 SU 67 SW Area centred SU 632713
ENGLEFIELD and THEALE
Incomplete rectangular enclosure.
NMR 70 SU 6370/4/441.

6371 6372 SU 67 SW Area centred SU
631721
ENGLEFIELD
Intersecting linear features.
NMR 70 SU 6372/5/413, 415.

6371 6372 SU 67 SW Area centred SU
638721
THEALE
Irregular linear features or incomplete
enclosures.
NMR 70 SU 6372/5/413, 415.

6372 SU 67 SW Area centred SU 635726
THEALE
Extensive complex of linear features,
rectangular enclosures and trackways.
NMR 70 SU 6372/2/, /3/396, 398, /4/400,
405, /6/417, 419, 421.

Map 8

6067 SU 66 NW Area centred SU 604678
BEENHAM
Single circle.
ST JOSEPH 58 WS 41-42.
RM 63 CM 116, 127.
Rescue excavation in 1963 showed the
ditch to be 180 feet in diameter. The
ditch was 0 feet wide and contained late
Neolithic pottery in the fill. (BAJ 1964,
61, p.99).
Site now totally destroyed by gravel
quarrying.

6067 6068 SU 66 NW Area centred SU
605681 BEENHAM
Parallel lines, trackways, linear features and
2 incomplete rectangular enclosures.
Large trapezoidal enclosure with heavily
marked edges and central block mark
(possibly an old gravel pit ?). Block mark.
Scattered pits.
ST JOSEPH 56 TD 44-45.
RM 63 CM 109, 117.
Site in process of destruction by gravel
quarrying. In 1974 a series of ditches,
flint-and mortar wall footings and a timber-
lined culvert, all belonging to the Romano-
British period, were briefly observed during
destruction in the vicinity of 605680.

6167 6267 SU 66 NW Area centred SU
620676   UFTON NERVET
2 circles. Trackways and linear features
to E.
ST JOSEPH 62 AFV 41.

6168 SU 66 NW Area centred SU 614686
BEENHAM
Parallel lines. Irregular enclosure. Block
mark.
NMR 70 SU 6269/5/33.

6168 SU 66 NW Area centred SU 617687
UFTON NERVET
3 irregular enclosures. Single circle. Block
marks. Trackway running SE-NW
NMR 70 SU 6269/5/35, 37.

6168 6169 SU 66 NW Area centred SU 617690
UFTON NERVET Pl. 4
Subrectangular enclosure partially divided by
linear feature and with internal pits. To SW
rectangular enclosure with entrance in W corner
leading into wide trackway running to SE.
Trackway passes to E of central enclosure and
leads to NW. Adjoining NE side of trackway
is a double-ditched rectangular enclosure.
Linear features or incomplete enclosures to
SW of complex. Scattered pits.
ST JOSEPH 56 TD 30; 60 ABX 49; 61 ADN 39,
44; 70 BCH 71-72.
NMR 69 SU 6169/3/70, /4/57, 59; 70 SU 6169/
8/9, 14,/9/27, 29.
RM 61 CM 106.
Excavations in 1961-2 by Manning showed the
central subrectangular enclosure to be of late
Iron Age date, and the double-ditched rectangular
enclosure to have been in use during the first
and second centuries AD. A single Saxon
Grubenhaus was also identified. (see BAJ 1961,
59, p.57-8; BAJ 1962, 60, p. 116-7; Journ. of
Roman Studies 1963, 53, p. 149;
Journ. of Roman Studies 1964, 55,
p. 172; and forthcoming publication in BAJ).

6169 SU 66 NW Area centred SU 614692
UFTON NERVET
Junction of 2 trackways. Linear features.
Small penannular enclosure.
NMR 69 SU 6169/3/72, 74; 70 SU 6169/9/24.
RM 61 CM 106.

6169 SU 66 NW Area centred SU 615695
UFTON NERVET
Extensive complex of curvilinear features. 7
circles and 2 conjoined circles.
Subrectangular enclosure. Block mark. Linear
feature at 617698.
ST JOSEPH 57 VG 33, VP 69; 61 ADN 36, 40;
70 BCH 74.
NMR 69 SU 6169/2/65, 67,/3/72, 74-75, 77;
70 SU 6169/7/474, 476, 478,/8/3, 5, 7,/9/20, 24

6169 6269 SU 66 NW Area centred SU 620693
UFTON NERVET Pl. 4
Road aligned SSE-NNW with trackway branching
off to NNE and leading to complex of rectangu-
lar enclosures and linear features.
ST JOSEPH 57 VP 69; 61 ADN 40; 70 BCH 77.
NMR SU 6169/2/62,/4/61; 70 SU 6169/7/480,
482; 71 SU 6169/10/129, 131.
RM 61 CM 106.

6267 6268 SU 66 NW Area centred SU 625682
UFTON NERVET
Linear features. Possible rectangular enclosure.
NMR 70 SU 6267/1/138, 140; 70 SU 6268/5.

6267 6367 6268 6368 SU 66 NW Area centred
SU 630682   UFTON NERVET
Complex with central group of 4 conjoined
rectangular enclosures. Further rectangular enclosures and linear features to NW. Possible

trackways and curvilinear features.
ST JOSEPH 62 AFV 38.
NMR 70 SU 6267/1/138, 140; 70 SU
6268/1, /4; 70 SU 6367/2; 70 SU 6368/2/
141,/3/147,149.

6269 6369 SU 66 NW Area centred
SU 627695. SULHAMSTEAD
Trackways and linear features. 2 small
circles. Small rectangular enclosure with
internal pit. Oval enclosure. Linear
features to E.
NMR 70 SU 6269/2/438,/3/439,/5/44,
46-48.

6269 6369 SU 66 NW Area centred SU
629699 ENGLEFIELD
Possible rectangular enclosure and adjoining
linear features. Parallel lines at 632699
(see *Map* 7 square 6370).
NMR 70 SU 6269/5/51.

6368 SU 66 NW Area centred SU 636683
SULHAMSTEAD
Linear features.
NMR 70 SU 6368/2/143.

6368 SU 66 NW Area centred SU 633687
SULHAMSTEAD
Possible rectangular enclosure and linear
features.
NMR 70 SU 6368/3/144, 146.

Map 9

6775 SU 67 NE Area centred SU 679753
MAPLEDURHAM
Rectangular enclosure with parallel linear
feature on E side.
NMR 70 SU 6775/1/387.
PRN 9703.

6774 SU 67 SE Area centred SU 686749
MAPLEDURHAM
Single circle. 5 pits.
ST JOSEPH 48 AP 17.
PRN 9704.

6875 SU 67 NE Area centred SU 682751
MAPLEDURHAM
Single circle.
NMR 69 SU 6875/1/182.
PRN 9705.

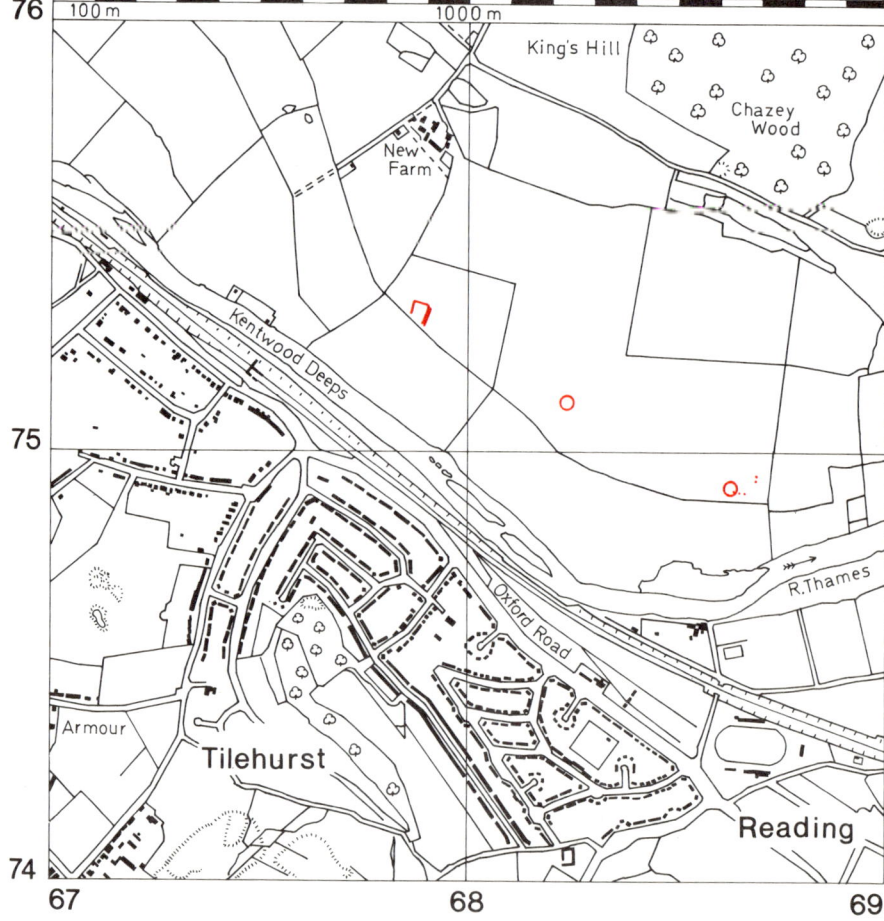

Map 9. Cropmarks southeast of Mapledurham

Map 10

6469 SU 66 NW Area centred SU 643695
BURGHFIELD
Single circle.
NMR 70 SU 6469/1/52.

6470 6570 6569 SU 67 SW, SE, 66 NE
Area centred SU 651702 BURGHFIELD
Complex of large enclosures, linear features
and trackways.
ST JOSEPH 61 ADN 30-31.
NMR 70 SU 6569/1/55-58.
Site totally destroyed by gravel quarrying
without investigation.

6570 6670 SU 67 NE Area centred
SU 660704 BURGHFIELD
Single circle. Intersecting linear features
and isolated curvilinear features. Pit.
Isolated linear feature and pit to S.
Whole area covered by small 'spots'.
ST JOSEPH 57 VP 66-67.
NMR 70 SU 6670/5/76-81.
Trial excavations in 1974 showed the
linear features to be field boundary
ditches of recent date. The pit at 671702
was an infilled medieval gravel pit or pond.
The 'spots' are caused by natural clay
patches lying on the gravel surface. Site
now totally destroyed by gravel quarrying.

6670 6669 SU 66 NE, 67 NE Area centred SU
664701   BURGHFIELD
Complex of intersecting linear features (land
drains?). 2 circles. 2 rectangular enclosures,
one with internal division, at NW of complex.
Isolated linear features to E at 668701.
ST JOSEPH 57 VP 65, 68; 70 BCH 78-79.
NMR 70 SU 6670/4/59-64.

6670 SU 67 NE Area centred SU 667708
BURGHFIELD
Branching trackway running N-S. Trackway
further to E running E-W. Incomplete rectilinear
enclosure and linear features.
NMR 70 SU 6670/4/65-75.
Features truncated by M4 construction in 1970.

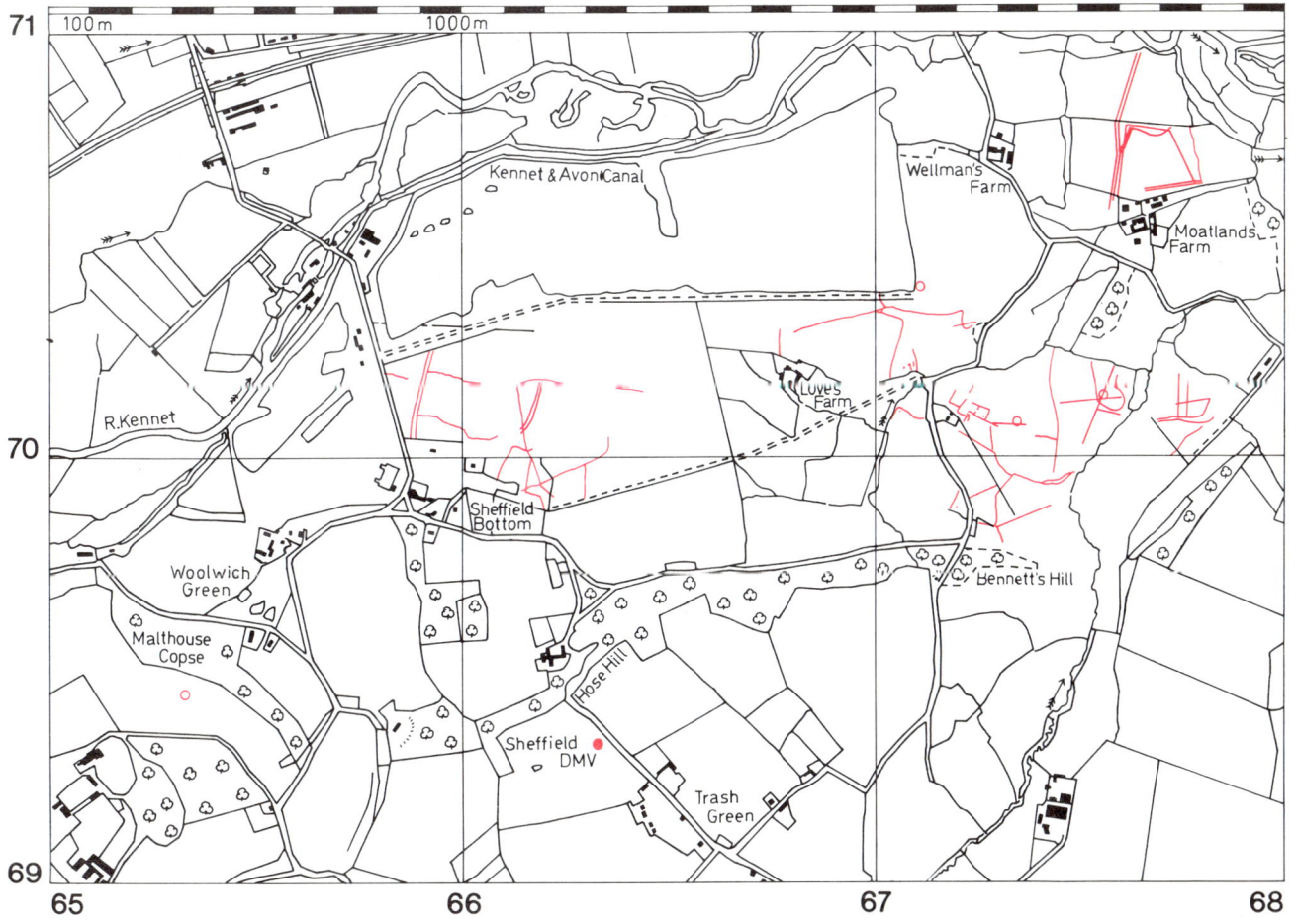

Map 10. Cropmarks between Theale and Burghfield

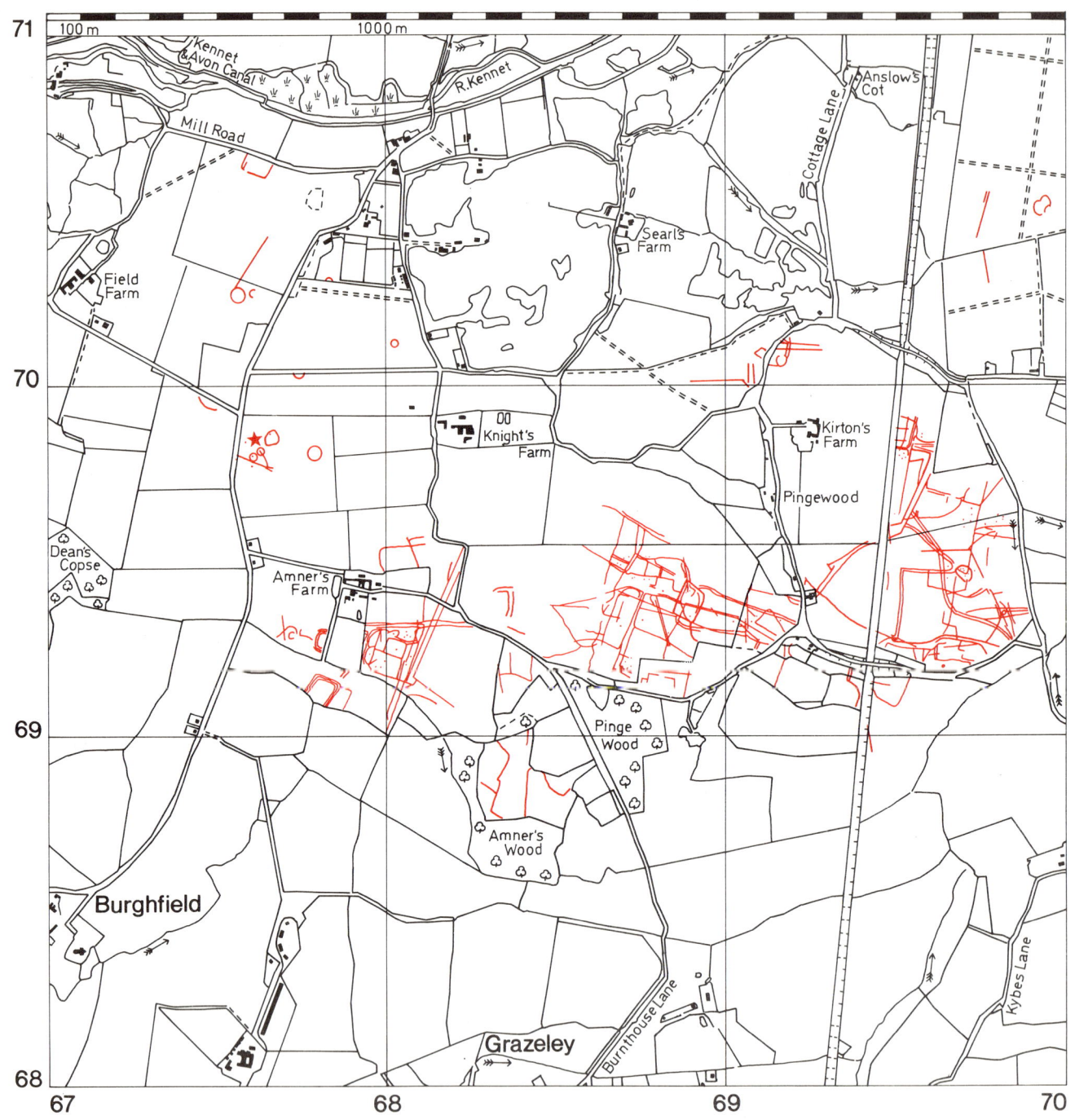

Map 11. Cropmarks northeast of Burghfield

Map 11

6769 SU 66 NE Area centred SU 678692
BURGHFIELD
Triple-ditched enclosure with single-ditched enclosure on E side. Parallel lines. Incomplete triple-ditched enclosure at 678693. To W irregular curvilinear and linear features and penannular enclosure.
ST JOSEPH 62 AFV 47-48.

6769 SU 66 NE Area centred SU 677698
BURGHFIELD
2 small circles and irregular oval enclosure with scattered pits and intersecting linear features. To E large circle. To NW curvilinear feature and pit.
ST JOSEPH 57 VP 58, 60-63; 60 ABX 39; 61 ADN 26, 28-29; 70 BCH 81.
Excavations in 1969 by Reading Museum of the two small ring-ditches failed to provide conclusive dating evidence though part of a horseshoe-handled pot (Bronze Age) was found in the fill of one ditch. The smaller ditch was 24 metres in diameter and the other slightly larger. No internal features were identified. These two ring-ditches were destroyed by the construction of the M4 in 1970. The remainder of the site was destroyed by gravel quarrying in 1973-4 without further investigation though the large circle at 678698 was identified during topsoil stripping and found to be 45 metres in diameter. Ironically a photograph of the site was published in *A Matter of Time* (HMSO 1960, plate 6a).

6770 SU 67 SE Area centred SU 677701
BURGHFIELD
Incomplete circle.
ST JOSEPH 57 VP 58, 60; 60 ABX 42; 61 ADN 26.
Site destroyed by gravel quarrying without investigation.

6770 SU 67 SE Area centred SU 676703
BURGHFIELD
Single circle and incomplete circle with tangential linear feature.
ST JOSEPH 60 ABX 39; 61 ADN 25, 27; 70 BCH 80.
NMR 70 6770/1/85, 88.

6770 SU 67 SE Area centred SU 678703
BURGHFIELD
Incomplete circle.
ST JOSEPH 61 ADN 27; 70 BCH 80.
NMR 70 SU 6770/1/85, 88.

6770 SU 67 SE Area centred SU 676706
BURGHFIELD
Rectangular enclosure with entrance on S side. Ridge and furrow.
NMR 70 SU 6770/1/88

6868 SU 66 NE Area centred SU 684689
BURGHFIELD
Irregular linear features (field boundary ditches and drains ?).
NMR 70 SU 6868/1/109,111

6769 6869 SU 66 NE Area centred SU 680692
BURGHFIELD *PL 5*
Settlement complex with central rectangular enclosure surrounded by curvilinear and rectilinear features. Complex bounded on N and E sides by trackways. Scattered pits. Further incomplete enclosure and linear features to N at 680695.
ST JOSEPH 62 AFV 47-48.

6869 6969 SU 66 NE Area centred SU 688693   BURGHFIELD *PL 6*
Extensive complex of intersecting trackways aligned SE-NW and NE-SW. Rectangular enclosures and linear features. Central subrectangular enclosure. Scattered pits. Linear features and parallel lines to W probably indicating that settlement extends further in that direction.
ST JOSEPH 69 AYH 40-41; 70 BCH 85, 87-88.
NMR 70 SU 6969/1/91,93-94,96-97,99, 101.
North edge of site damaged by construction of M4 in 1970 and subsequent gravel quarrying.

6870 SU 67 SE Area centred SU 681701
BURGHFIELD
Single circle.
ST JOSEPH 60 ABX 42; 61 ADN 25.
NMR 70 SU 6770/1/85, 88.

6969 SU 66 NE Area centred SU 697695
BURGHFIELD *PL 7 & 8*
Extensive complex of intersecting trackways, linear features and enclosures. Central D-shaped enclosure at 69706944 containing many pits. 2 small circles. Scattered pits.
ST JOSEPH 69 AYH 43-44; 70 BCH 82-84.
NMR 70 SU 6969/1/103, 105, 108; 71 SU 6969/8/179,/10/182; 72 SU 6969/12/91, 94,/14/98, 100, 102, 104,/15/106, 108.
Site badly damaged during M4 construction in 1970 (see *Plates 7 & 8*) without prior investigation.

6870 6970 SU 67 SE Area centred SU 691701   BURGHFIELD
Rectangular enclosure, penannular enclosure, linear features and parallel lines.
ST JOSEPH 61 ADN 23-24.
Site totally destoryed by gravel quarrying without investigation.

6970 SU 67 SE Area centred SU 699704
READING
2 conjoined subcircular enclosures. To W linear features and parallel lines.
ST JOSEPH 61 ADN 22.

Map 12

7265 SU 76 NW Area centred SU 722654
SWALLOWFIELD
Single circle.
ST JOSEPH 70 BCW 17.

7265 7266 SU 76 NW Area centred SU 722659
SWALLOWFIELD
Settlement complex with 3 rectangular enclosures, 5 small circles (hut emplacements ?), trackways and linear features.
ST JOSEPH 59 AAL 7; 70 BCW 12, 14.

7266 7267 SU 76 NW Area centred SU 727670
SHINFIELD
Linear features (recent drainage ditches ?).
NMR 70 SU 7267/2, 3.

Map 12. Cropmarks around Spencers Wood

34

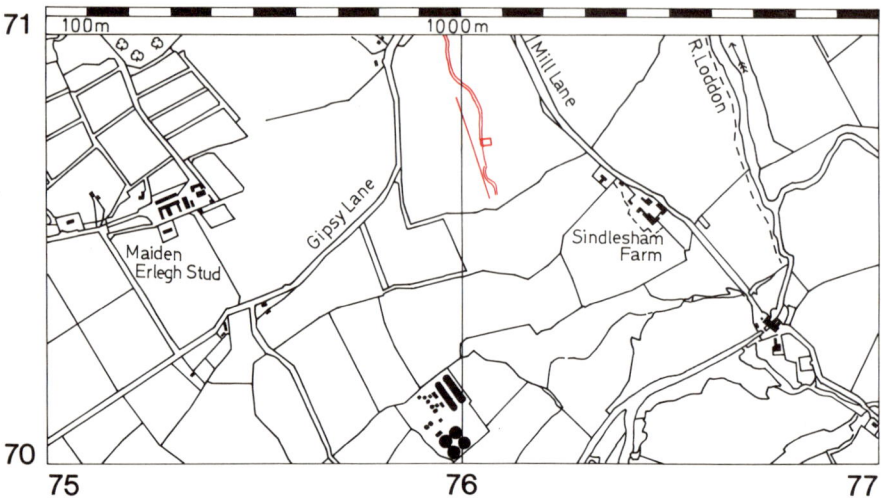

Map 13. Cropmarks south of Earley

Map 13

7570 7670 SU 77 SE Area centred
SU 760708 WOODLEY and SANDFORD
Rectangular enclosure and curvilinear trackway running approximately N-S. Linear
feature to W of trackway. Trackway
continues for 140 metres off the north
edge of the map.
NMR 69 SU 7670/1,/2/20,/4/23, 25, 27,
29,/5/31.

Map 14

7367 SU 76 NW Area centred SU 738677
SHINFIELD
Incomplete rectangular enclosures.
Trackway and linear features.
BAU 74

7368 SU 76 NW Area centred SU 738686
SHINFIELD
Subrectangular enclosure with entrance on
SE side. Linear features. Trackway.
Probable river meanders (not plotted).
ST JOSEPH 59 YN 93-94.

7468 SU 76 NW Area centred SU 746682
SHINFIELD
Single circle.
BAU 74

7469 SU 76 NW Area centred SU 743697
SHINFIELD
2 rectangular enclosures. Parallel lines and
linear features.
ST JOSEPH 59 YN 95.

7567 SU 76 NE Area centred SU 756672
ARBORFIELD and NEWLAND
Parallel lines. Incomplete rectangular
enclosure. Linear features.
NMR 70 SU 7567/1.

7567 7568 SU 76 NE Area centred
SU 752681
ARBORFIELD and NEWLAND
Junction of 2 roads. Rectangular en-
closure. Parallel lines and intersecting
linear features. Scattered pits.
NMR 70 SU 7568/1, 2, 4.

7568 SU 76 NE Area centred SU 757683
ARBORFIELD and NEWLAND
Complex of linear features and
rectangular enclosures. Old water-
courses or drainage ditches ?
NMR 70 SU 7568/7, 9, 10.

7568 SU 76 NE Area centred SU 755687
ARBORFIELD and NEWLAND
Isolated linear features.
BAU 74

7568 7569 SU 76 NE Area centred
SU 758690
ARBORFIELD and NEWLAND
2 rectangular enclosures, including one
with double ditches. Parallel lines and
linear features.
ST JOSEPH 70 BCW 22-23
NMR 70 7568/11/3,/12/4, 7.
BAU 74

7569 SU 76 NE Area centred SU 754694
EARLEY
Incomplete rectangular enclosures and
single pit.
BAU 74

7669 SU 76 NE Area centred SU 763695
ARBORFIELD and NEWLAND
Single circle crossed by linear feature.
Periglacial features (not plotted).
BAU 74.

Map 15

7263 SU 76 SW Area centred SU 728636
SWALLOWFIELD
Linear features. Incomplete rectangular
enclosure at 728635.
NMR 70 SU 7263/1, 2, 4.
    The Silchester to London Roman road, known
as the Devil's Highway, crosses the bottom of
the map and is marked by the straight stretch
of road in squares 7263 and 7363.

7363 SU 76 SW Area centred SU 732634
SWALLOWFIELD
Intersecting linear features. Parallel lines
(possibly a road ?). Five-sided enclosure
containing small circle. Possible enclosure.
NMR 70 SU 7363/1-3.

7363 SU 76 SW Area centred SU 734635
SWALLOWFIELD
Settlement complex with rectangular
enclosure, 2 suboval enclosures. 7 small
circles (hut emplacements ?). Incomplete
double concentric circle. Trackway and
intersecting linear features.
ST JOSEPH 62 AFW 24-25.
NMR 70 SU 7363/4, 5

7363 SU 76 SW Area centred SU 737637
SWALLOWFIELD
Linear features and curvilinear features.
ST JOSEPH 62 AFW 24-25.

7363 7364 SU 76 SW Area centred SU 733639
SWALLOWFIELD
Subrectangular enclosure with entrance on S side
within second incomplete enclosure.
Parallel lines and linear features to N and W.
ST JOSEPH 61 ADN 82, 84.

7264 7364 SU 76 SW Area centred SU 730645
SWALLOWFIELD *Pl. 9*
2 rectangular enclosures with entrances on S
side, including one with possible internal hut
emplacements. Single small circle with
adjacent pit. Intersecting linear features

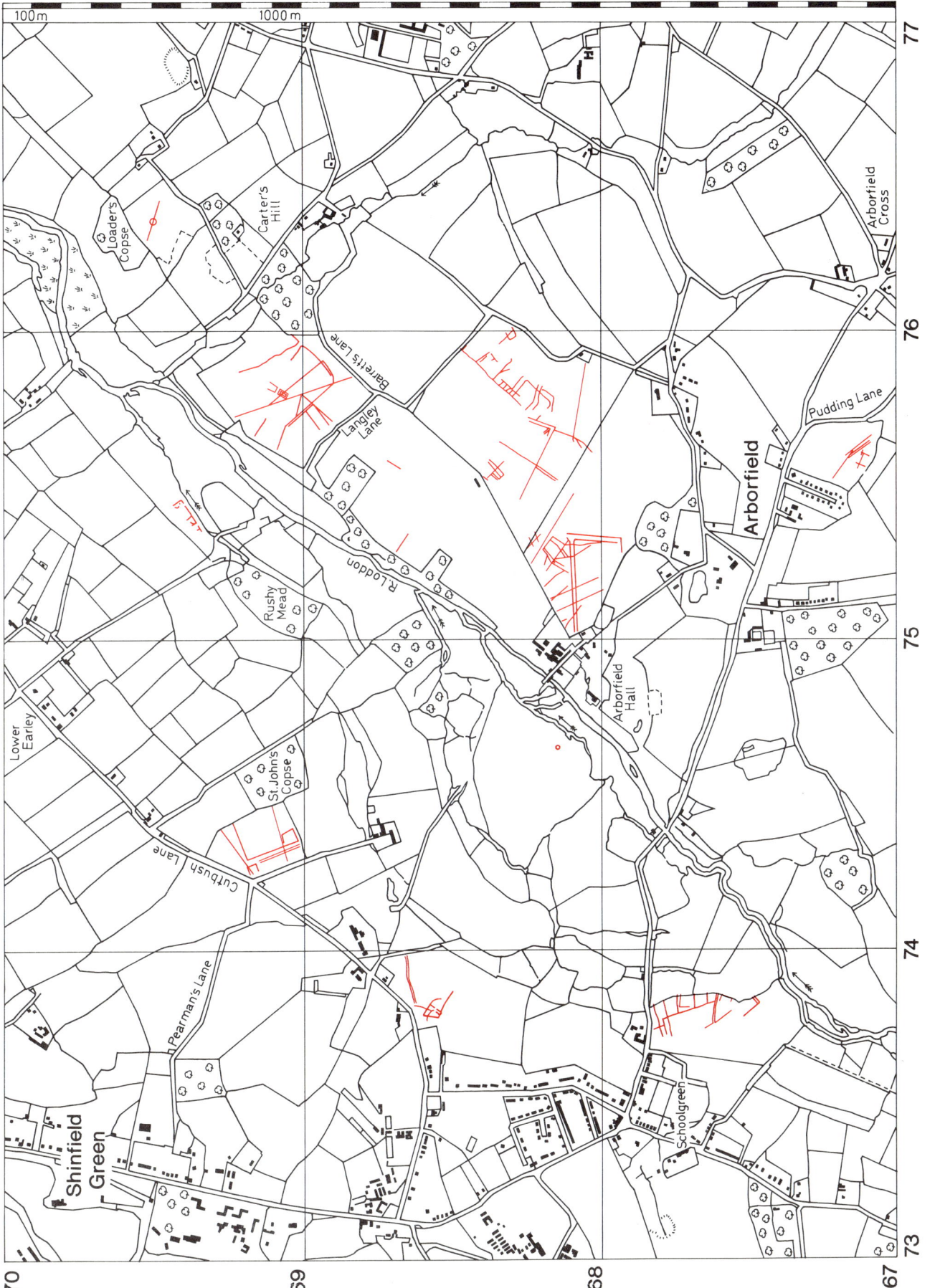

Map 14. Cropmarks around Shinfield and Arborfield

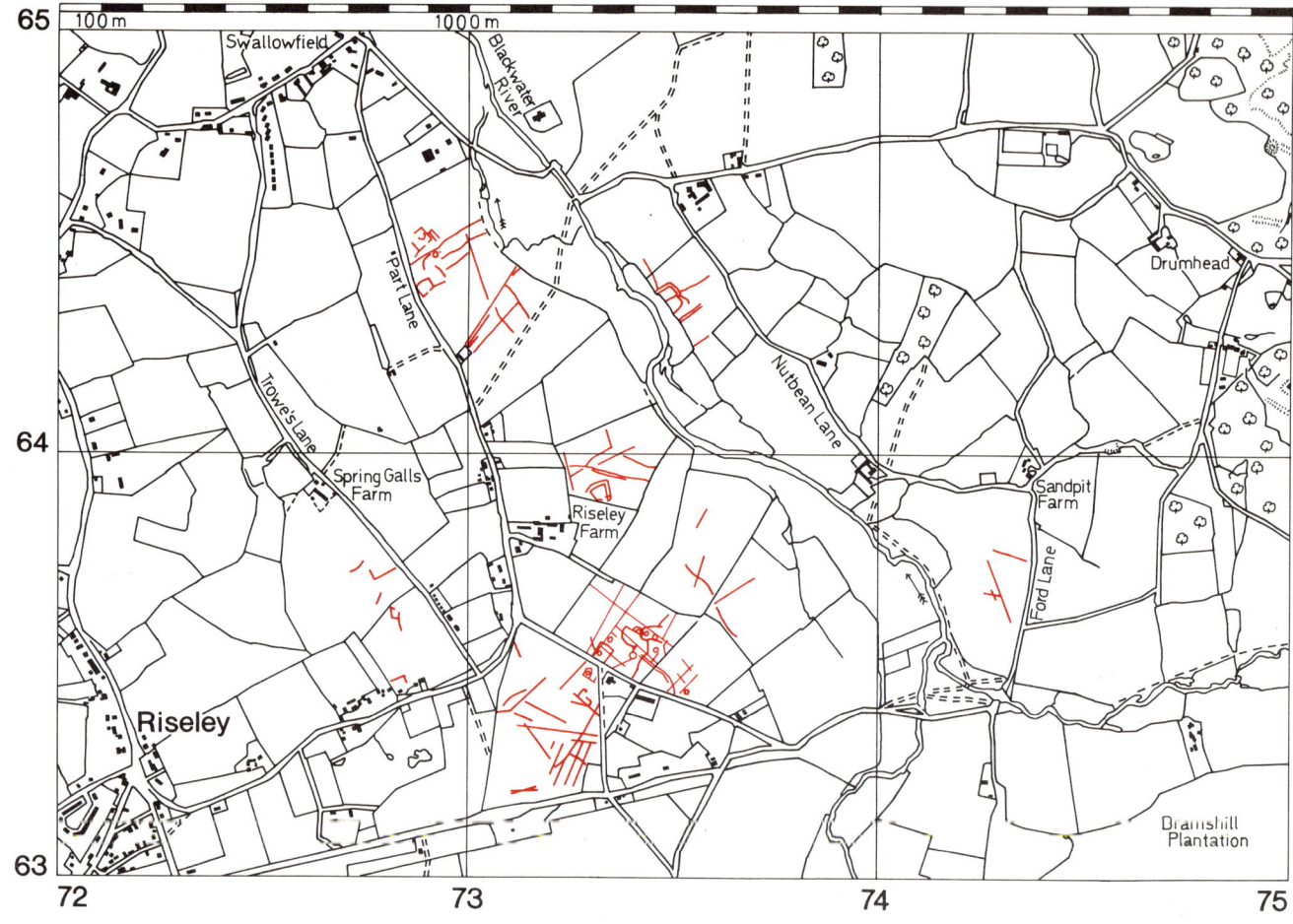

Map 15. Cropmarks around Swallowfield and Riseley

(Map 15 continued)
and parallel lines.
ST JOSEPH 70 BCW 15-16.

7364 SU 76 SW Area centred SU 735644
SWALLOWFIELD
2 incomplete subrectangular enclosures.
Parallel lines. Linear features.
ST JOSEPH 62 AFW 20.
NMR 70 SU 7364/1-3.

7463 SU 76 SW Area centred SU 742637
SWALLOWFIELD
Linear features.
NMR 70 SU 7463/1.

Map 16

7476 SU 77 NW Area centred SU 749767
EYE and DUNSDEN
Single circle with internal pit. Linear
features (possibly old watercourses).
NMR 70 SU 7476/1/50.

7576 SU 77 NE Area centred SU 755767
EYE and DUNSDEN
Group of 4 circles. Curvilinear feature,
double in part. To SE subrectangular en-
closure and pits.
ST JOSEPH 70 BCW 28.
NMR 69 SU 7576/1/59, 62.

7577 SU 77 NE Area centred SU 756772
EYE and DUNSDEN
Parallel lines. To E single circle.
BAU 74

Map 17

7777 SU 77 NE Area centred SU 779774
WARGRAVE
Single small circle. To N oval enclosure
with internal division.
ST JOSEPH 59 YO 13; 62 AFW 16.

7877 SU 77 NE Area centred SU 781773
WARGRAVE
2 small circles and linear feature.
ST JOSEPH 59 YO 13.

7877 SU 77 NE Area centred SU 781778
WARGRAVE *pl. 10*
Settlement complex with rectangular enclosure
with entrance on W side. Linear features.
Possible incomplete enclosures. Many pits.
Single circle to W. Open-ended rectangular
feature to N.
ST JOSEPH 59 YO 11.
RM 59 CM 16.

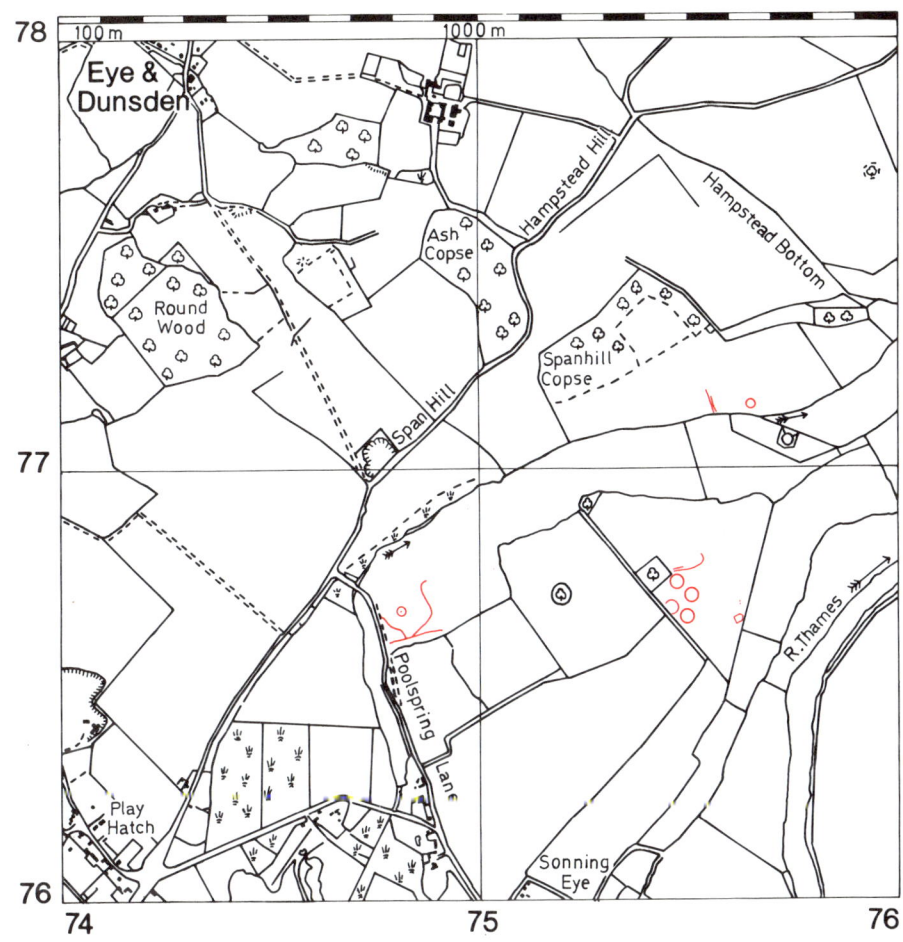

Map 16. Cropmarks southwest of Shiplake

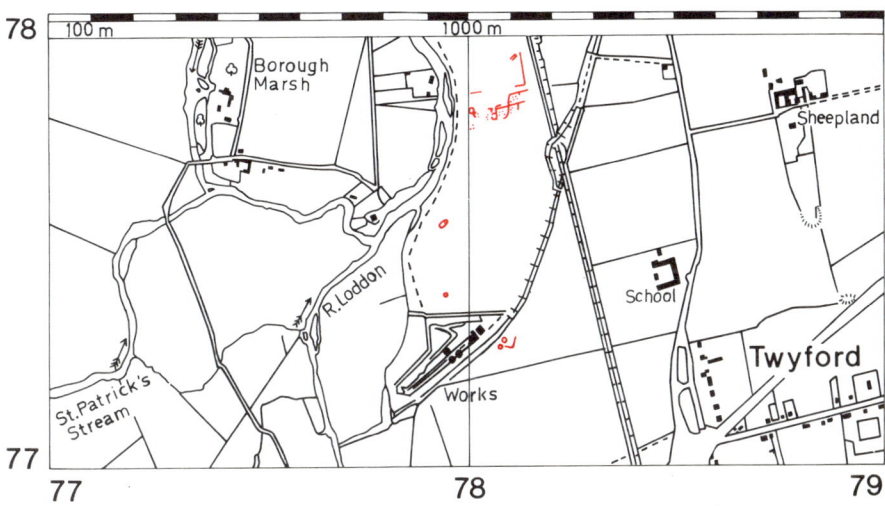

Map 17. Cropmarks southeast of Wargrave

Map 18

7375 SU 77 NW Area centred SU 738759
EYE and DUNSDEN
Single circle.
NMR 72 SU 7375/1/99.

Map 19

7675 SU 77 NE Area centred SU 766755
SONNING
3 circles, one with internal pit. Enclosure
with internal circle. Trackway. Complex
of linear and curvilinear features, some
possibly of periglacial origin or representing
old watercourses.
ST JOSEPH 59 YO 1, 5; 61 ADN 20
Excavation of the ring ditch at 767756 in
1960 showed it to be 47 feet in diameter,
but no dateable material was recovered
(*BAJ* 1960, *58,* p.63).

7675 7676 SU 77 NE Area centred SU
766759 SONNING *Pl. 11*
Cursus 45 metres wide with entrance in E
end. To N 2 rectangular enclosures, single
circle and curvilinear ditch. To E single
small circle. To S polygonal enclosure
and trackway.
ST JOSEPH 59 YO 3, YN 97; 61 ADN 16;
67 ARW 52; 70 BCW 25.
NMR 70 SU 7676/1/55; 72 SU 7676/2/75,
77.
Excavation of the rectangular enclosure in
Straighthanger field at 767759 in 1959-62
showed it to be of Neolithic date. A
parallel with the apparently ritual enclosure
at Site I, Dorchester-on-Thames, has been
suggested (SLADE 1964).

7676 SU 77 NE Area centred SU 769762
SONNING and CHARVIL
Linear features. Elongated oval enclosure
to SW. To NE rectangular enclosure
with entrance on E side and internal
circle. Single small circle to E.
ST JOSEPH 62 AFV 50, AFW 18.
NMR 70 SU 7676/1/59; 72 SU 7676/2/79,
82.

7775 SU 77 NE Area centred SU 771754
SONNING
Group of 5 circles, including one double
concentric one, associated with a right-
angled linear feature. Possible traces of
further circles (not plotted).
ST JOSEPH 59 YO 2.

7776 SU 77 NE Area centred SU 773764
CHARVIL
Linear features. Small circle. To N
single circle with central pit.
ST JOSEPH 62 AFW 17; 70 BCW 24.
NMR 69 SU 7675/5/40; 72 SU 7676/2/84.

7776 SU 77 NE Area centred SU 772767
CHARVIL
Rectangular enclosure with entrance on NE
side and internal pits. Associated linear
features.
ST JOSEPH 52 YO 8-9.
NMR 69 SU 7776/1/393.

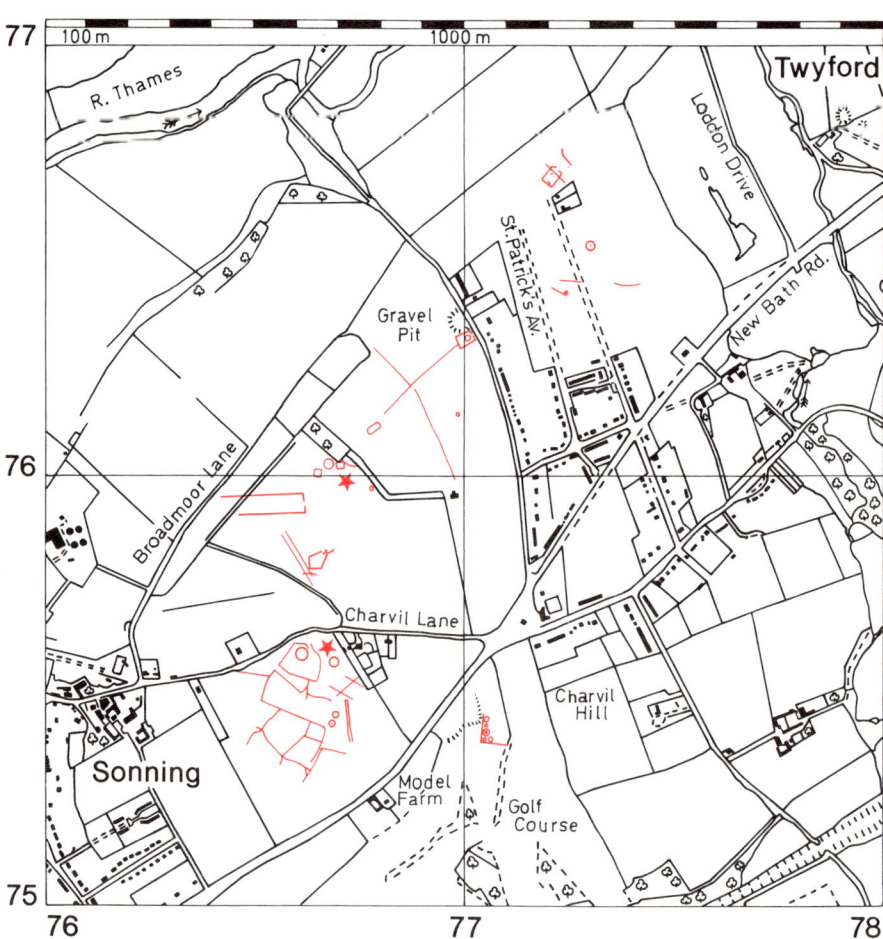

Map 18. Cropmark northeast of Caversham

Map 19. Cropmarks around Sonning

Map 20

7778 SU 77 NE Area Centred SU 778789
SHIPLAKE
2 superimposed irregular enclosures with
entrances on S side. Linear feature. Pits.
NMR 70 7778/2/63.
RM 59 CM 17.
PRN 2161.
   RB bricks, pottery and bones
found in Shiplake in 1907-9 (see
Berks., Bucks., & Oxon. Arch. Journ.,
1918, *24,* pp. 34-5).

7779 SU 77 NE Area centred SU 770791
SHIPLAKE
Small rectangular enclosure and pits.
NMR 70 SU 7779/1/61-62.

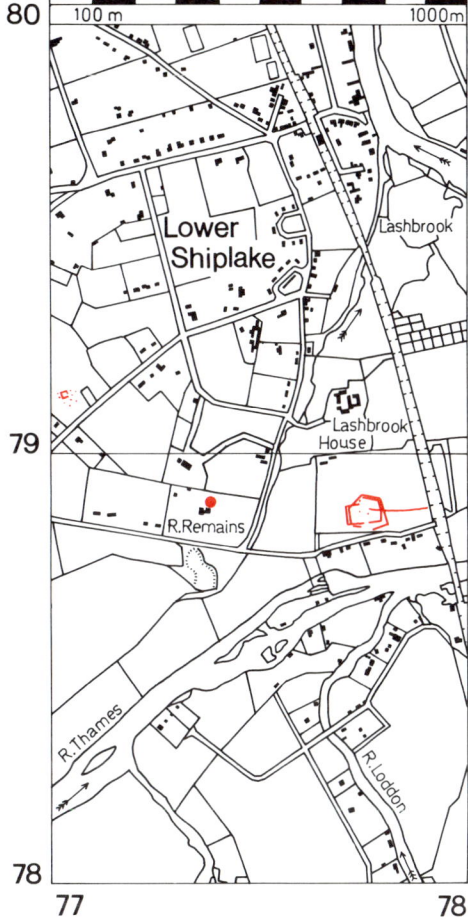

Map. 20 Cropmarks east of Shiplake

40

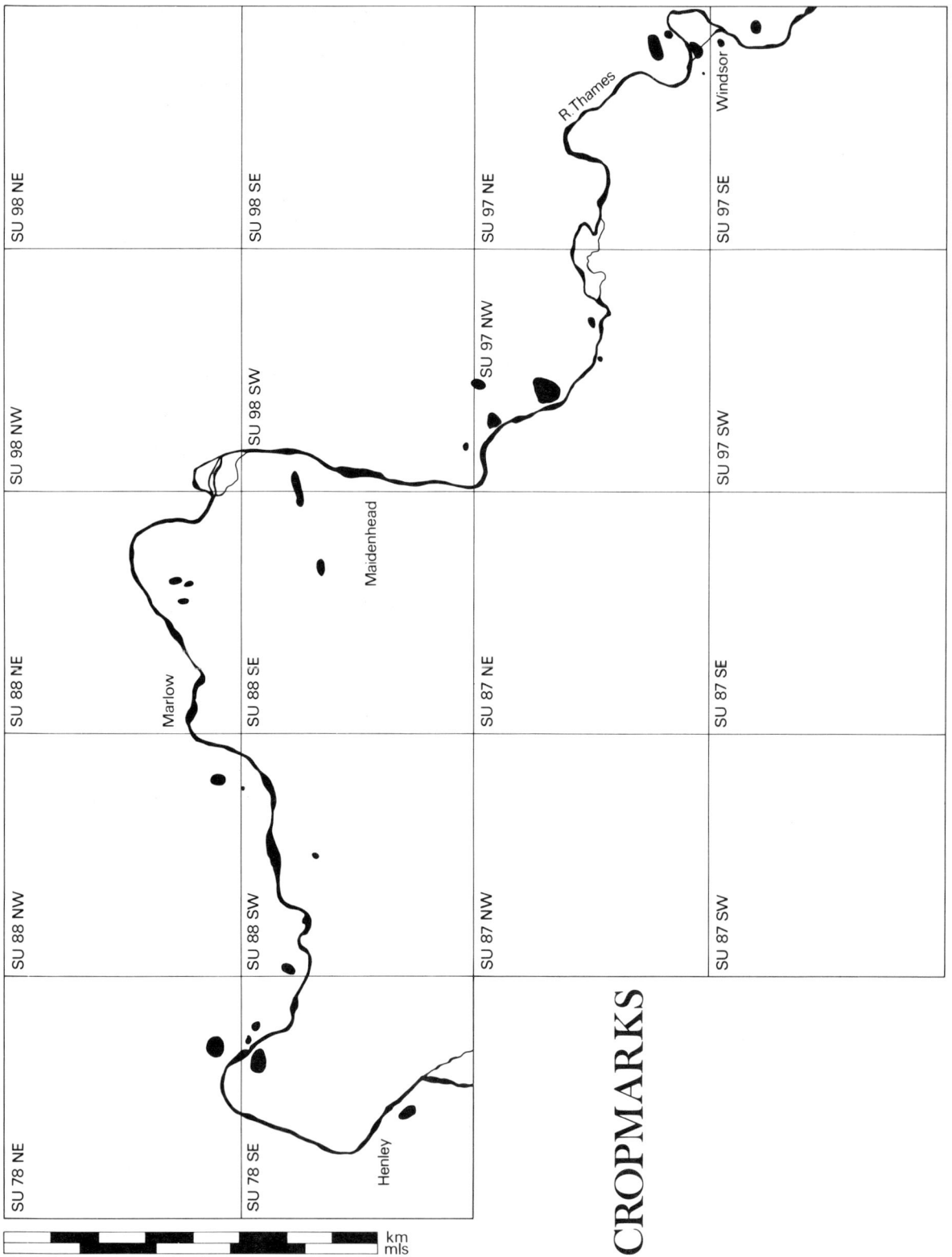

CROPMARKS

Fig. 6 Distribution of cropmarks in Section 2 Thames Valley Shiplake-Wraysbury

41

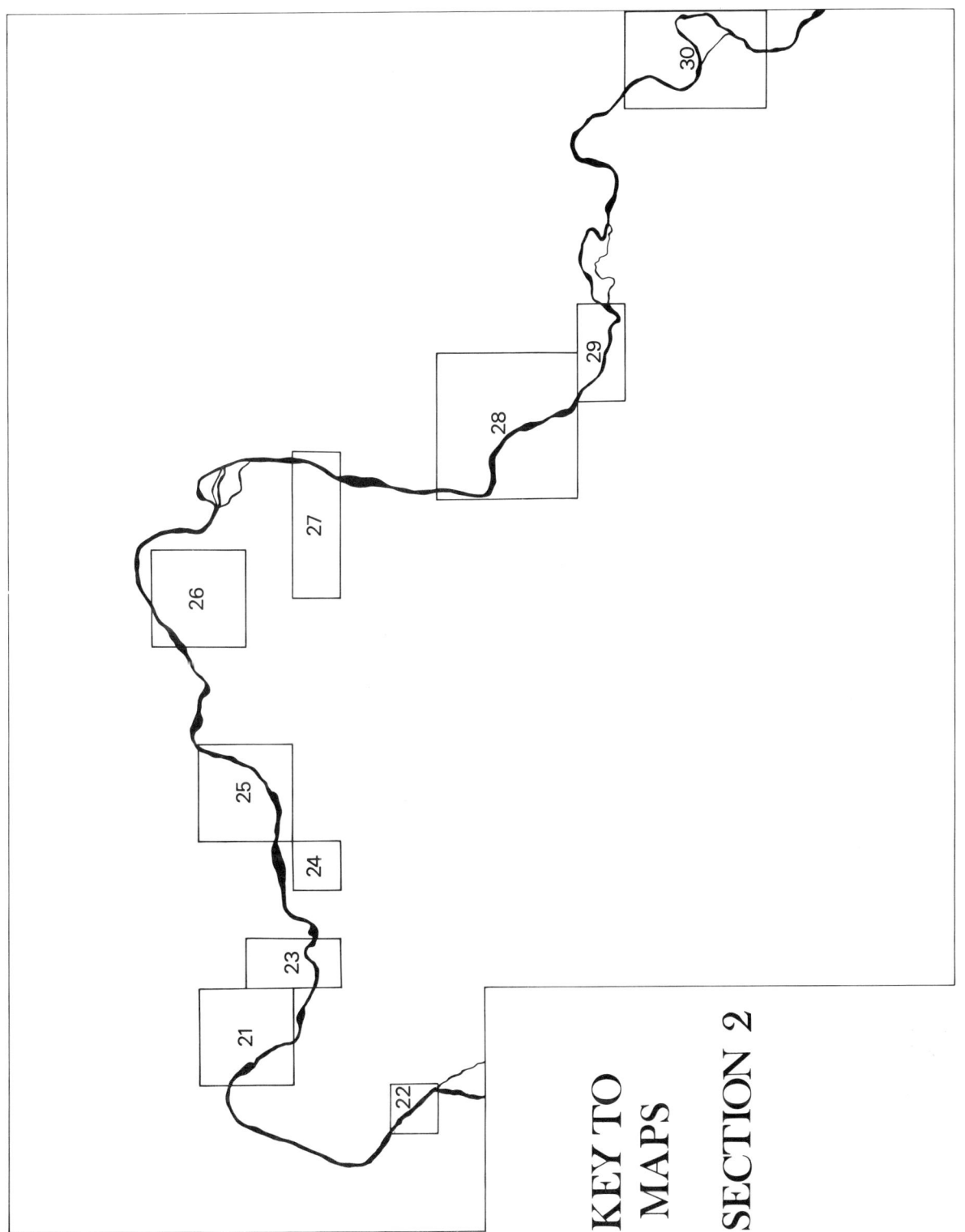

KEY TO
MAPS

SECTION 2

Fig. 7 Key to cropmark maps in Section 2

SECTION 2. CROPMARKS IN THE THAMES VALLEY BETWEEN SHIPLAKE AND WRAYSBURY

Map 21

7884 SU 78 SE Area centred SU 783846
REMENHAM
Complex of enclosures and linear features, probably representing a settlement and its enclosure system. Single circle. Block mark. Small rectangular enclosure and pits to W.
NMR 69 SU 7884/1/63,/2/66;
70 SU 7884/6/77.

7884 SU 78 SE Area centred SU 786848
HAMBLEDEN
E-shaped Roman villa (approx. 35m x 20m) opening to SW and overlooking the Thames. Parallel linear features to E.
NMR 70 SU 7884/8/84
Fragments of Roman pottery and tile have been recovered from the surface of the field which is now under pasture.

7884 7984 SU 78 SE Area centred
SU 789847   HAMBLEDEN
2 circles.
NMR 69 SU 7884/3/69.

7885 SU 78 NE Area centred SU 785856
HAMBLEDEN
Complex of enclosures, pits and linear features. To W Roman villa (40m x 30m) and parts of two associated rectangular buildings. To E at 786855 further linear features or enclosures.
NMR 70 SU 7885/3, 5.
Excavations in 1912 revealed an E-shaped Roman villa and two associated barns or workshops contained within a three-sided enclosure wall. An important series of grain drying ovens was also recorded. The site was apparently occupied from the first to the fourth centuries AD (COCKS 1921).

Map 22

7781 SU 78 SE Area centred SU 771814
HARPSDEN and HENLEY
Rectangular enclosure with entrance on NE side. Associated linear features and pits. Isolated linear feature to E. To N at 770816

small rectangular enclosure.
NMR 70 SU 7781/2/69.
PRN 9701-2.

Map 23

8083 8084 SU 88 SW Area centred SU 801840
MEDMENHAM
Small rectangular enclosure. Complex linear and curvilinear features. Single incomplete circle to S.
ST JOSEPH 62 AFW 12.

Map 24

8283 SU 88 SW Area centred SU 825834
HURLEY
Single circle with central pit. To N many small spots that could be natural subsoil features, pits or graves.
ST JOSEPH 59 YO 39.

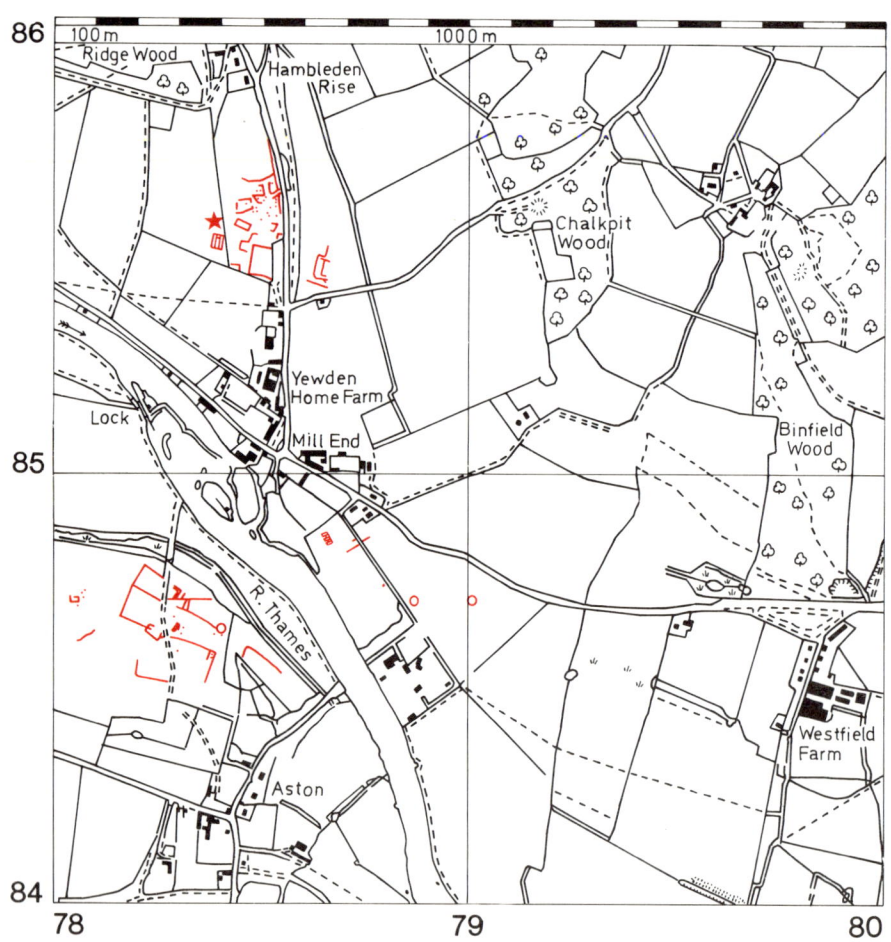

Map 21. Cropmarks around Mill End and Aston

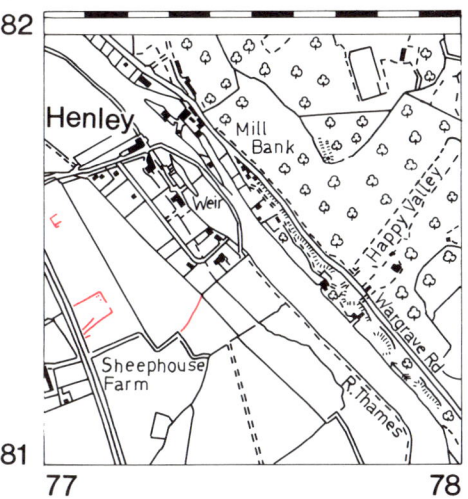

Map 22. Cropmarks east of Henley

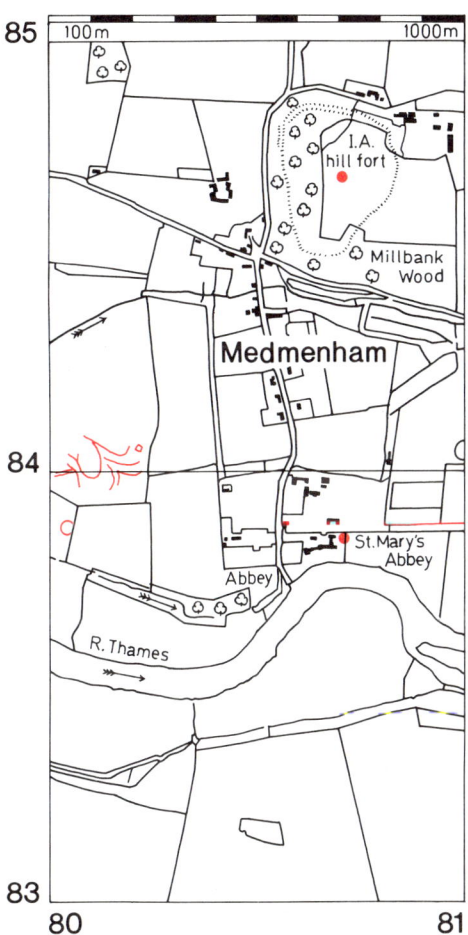

Map 23. Cropmarks at Medmenham

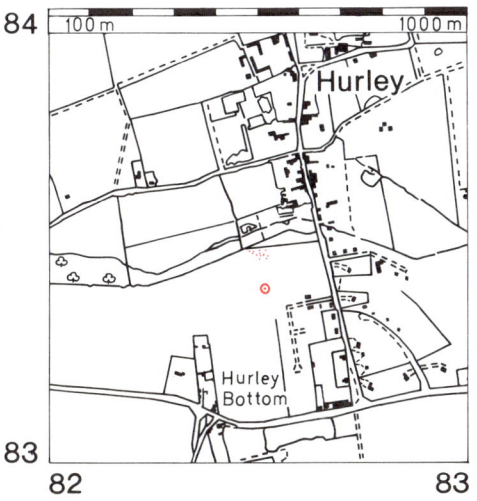

Map 24. Cropmarks at Hurley

44

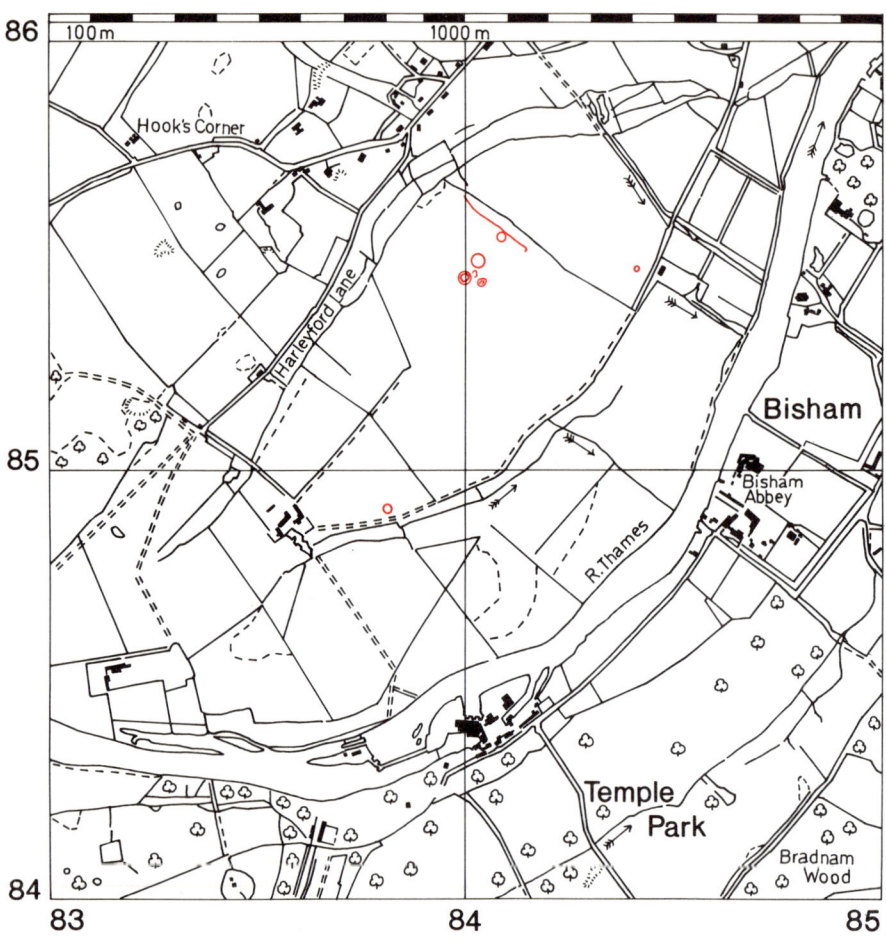

86

100 m   1000 m

Hook's Corner

Harleyford Lane

Bisham

85

Bisham Abbey

R.Thames

Temple Park

Bradnam Wood

84

83   84   85

Map 25. Cropmarks around Bisham

Map 25

8384 SU 88 SW Area centred SU 838849
MARLOW
Single circle.
ST JOSEPH 57 VP 29.
NMR 70 SU 8384/1.

8385 8485 SU 88 NW Area centred
SU 840855   MARLOW *Pl. 12*
Group of 3 circles, including one double
concentric circle. Subcircular enclosure
with internal feature (another enclosure ?).
Irregular enclosure. Linear feature adjacent
to NE circle.
ST JOSEPH 57 VP 30, 32; 59 YO 36, 38.
NMR 70 SU 8385/1/88, 90.

8485 SU 88 NW Area centred SU 844855
MARLOW
Single circle.
NMR 70 SU 8485/5/108.

Map 26

8786 SU 88 NE Area centred SU 877863
COOKHAM
Linear feature — possibly a recent field
boundary ditch. Penannular enclosure.
The area is covered by many small 'spots'
which may indicate natural subsoil features
(not plotted).
NMR SU 8786/2/103.

8885 8886 SU 88 NE Area centred
SU 881861   COOKHAM
Irregular enclosures. Small rectangular
enclosures and associated linear features,
possibly representing a settlement. The
area is covered by 'spots' similar to those
in 8786.
NMR 70 SU 8885/1/98.
Small Saxon cemetery with six inhu-
mations destroyed during railway construction in 1854 at SU 889858.

8886 SU 88 NE Area centred SU 881864
COOKHAM
Linear feature.
NMR 70 SU 8886/1/102.

Map 27

8883 SU 88 SE Area centred SU 884833
MAIDENHEAD
Incomplete enclosures including one with
in-turned entrance on W side. Linear features
and scattered pits. To NW 3 circles and pits.
ST JOSEPH 57 VP 25-27; 59 YO 17-18.
Rescue excavations from 1959 to 1960 in a
gravel pit at SU 886839 revealed RB occupation
from the first to fourth centuries AD. Finds
included a T-shaped kiln, and a well containing
an almost complete wooden writing tablet.
(*BAJ* 1959, *57*, p. 123; 1960, *58*, p.60).

8983 SU 88 SE Area centred SU 899838
MAIDENHEAD
Single circle. Incomplete enclosure.
Parallel lines (trackways?) and linear
features. Scattered pits ?
ST JOSEPH 59 YO 22-24.

9083 SU 98 SW Area centred SU 901838
MAIDENHEAD
Incomplete enclosure ?
ST JOSEPH 59 YO 22, 26.

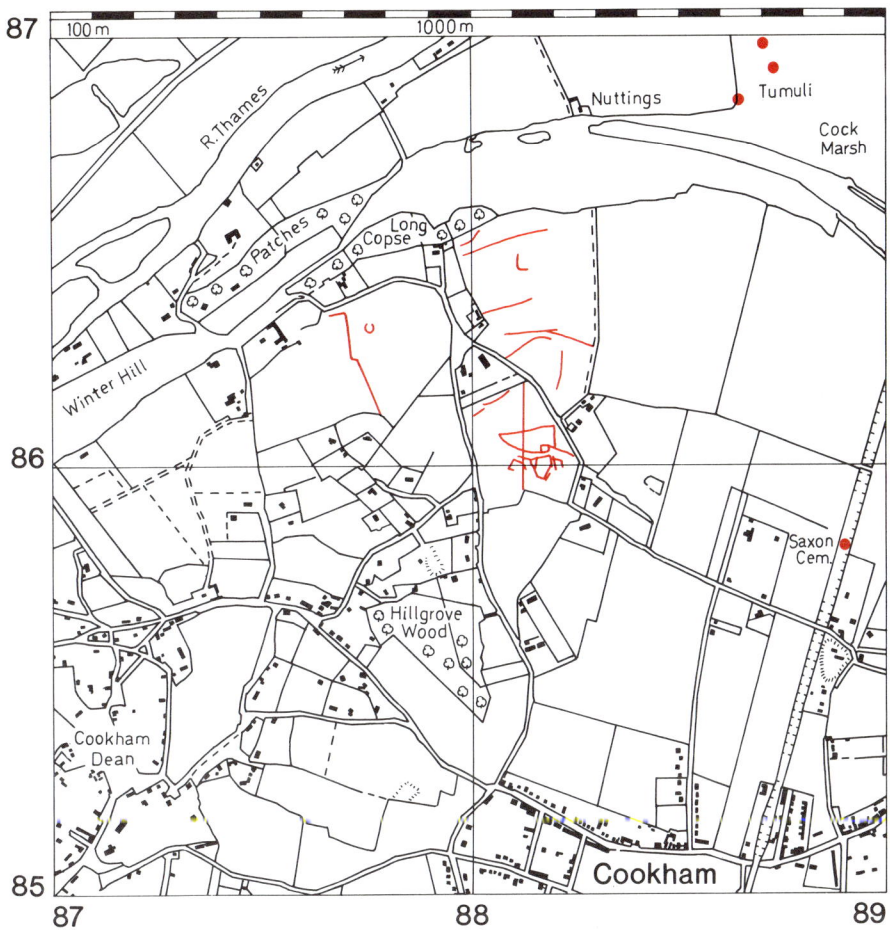

Map 26. Cropmarks northwest of Cookham

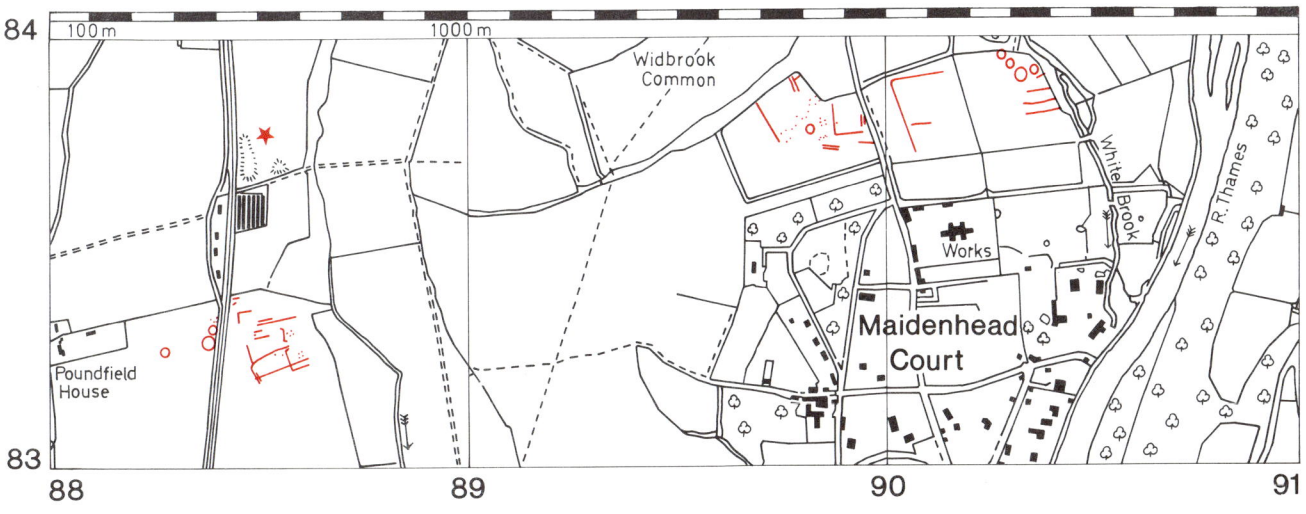

Map 27. Cropmarks north of Maidenhead

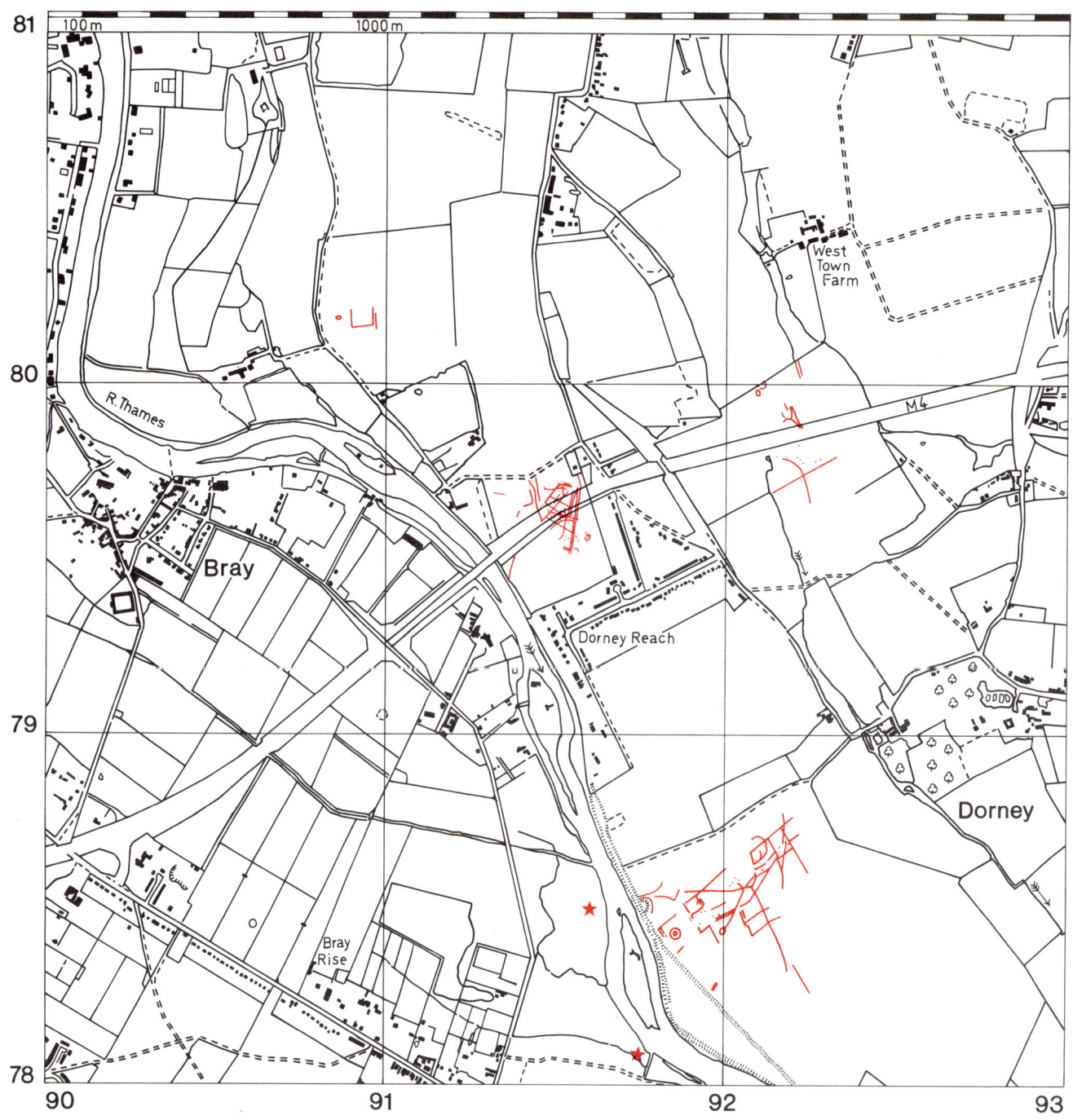

Map 28. Cropmarks around Bray and Dorney

(Map 27 continued)
9083 SU 98 SW Area centred SU 903839
MAIDENHEAD
4 circles. Parallel linear features.
ST JOSEPH 59 YO 25-26.

Map 28

9080 SU 98 Area centred SU 909802
TAPLOW
Incomplete rectangular enclosure with
adjacent linear feature. Small oval
enclosure immediately to W.
ST JOSEPH 57 VP 8-10.

9179 SU 97 NW Area centred SU 915796
TAPLOW
Settlement complex with rectilinear enclo-
sures, linear features and scattered pits.
2 trackways, one with junction. Single
circle in centre of complex. To SE oval
enclosure with entrance and internal pits.
Isolated linear features to W and S.
ST JOSEPH 57 VF 58, VP 12, 14, 20, 23,
24.
Site largely destroyed by construction of
M4 in 1970 without prior examination.

9279 9280 SU 97 NW, 98 SW Area
centred SU 922799   DORNEY
Incomplete circle. Small oval enclosure.
Parallel lines to N (trackway ?). Irregular
linear features to S. To S curvilinear feature
crossed by linear feature and scattered
pits.
ST JOSEPH 57 VF 56.
Site partially destroyed by construction
of M4 in 1970 without examination.

9178 9278 SU 97 NW Area centred SU
920785
DORNEY *Pl. 13*
Settlement complex with 4 subrectangular
enclosures and many incomplete ones.
Associated linear and curvilinear
features, parallel lines and scattered pits.
Small circle. To W at 91887840
large double concentric circle, diameters
30m and 15m.
Block mark to S. Ridge and furrow.
ST JOSEPH 57 VF 59, 61, VP 7; 59 YO
28-30.
Between 1962 and 1970 many finds of
Mesolithic, Neolithic, Bronze Age, Iron Age
and Roman date were recovered from the
screening plant in the Hoveringham gravel
pit at Monkey Island, Bray, on the south
bank of the Thames in the vicinity of
SU 915784. The finds included a
presumed hoard of ten middle to late
Bronze Age weapons. Rescue excavations
in the pit in 1966 recovered large quantities
of Iron Age pottery and bones from
SU 916785. Further excavations in 1970
at SU 918781 revealed Romano-British
occupation of the fourth and fifth
centuries AD (see *BAJ* 1962, *60*, p.115-6,
118; 1964, *61*, p.97, 99, 103-5; 1966,
62, p.72; 1970, *65*, p.57). The whole
area has now been totally destroyed by
gravel quarrying.

Map 29

9277 SU 97 NW Area centred SU 928773
BRAY
Single circle.
ST JOSEPH 59 YH 99.

9277 SU 97 NW Area centred SU 927779
DORNEY
Single circle. Rectangular enclosure. Pits
and linear features. Not plotted because
of the lack of landmarks on the aerial
photographs.
ST JOSEPH 59 YH 100, YO 32.

9377 SU 97 NW Area centred SU 934775
DORNEY
Circle with internal pit. Circle with
entrance on S side crossed by linear
feature.
Linear feature to NE.
ST JOSEPH 57 VF 62, VP 1-3; 59 YO
33.

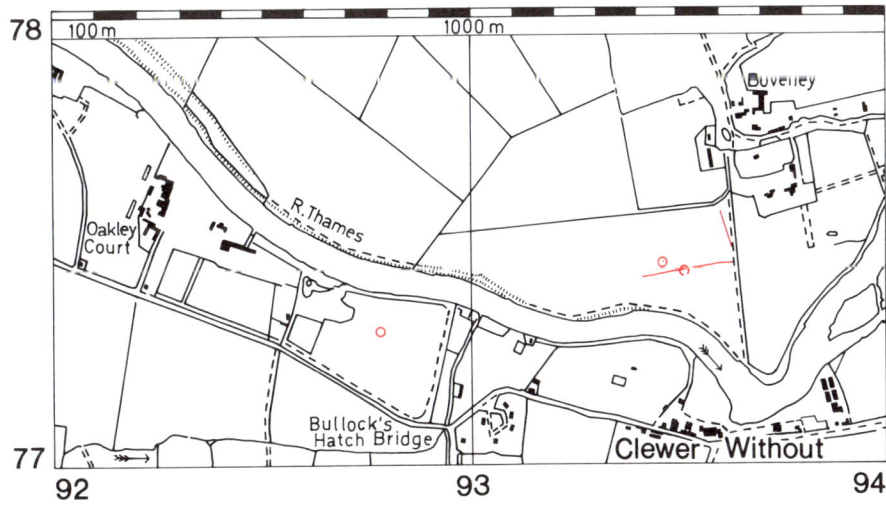

Map 29. Cropmarks south of Dorney

Map 30

9875 SU 97 NE Area centred SU 986751
OLD WINDSOR
Incomplete circle.
ST JOSEPH 57 VF 78.

9876 SU 97 NE Area centred SU 989762
DATCHET
Linear features.
ST JOSEPH 56 TH 82, 84.

9974 SU 97 SE Area centred SU 996741
WRAYSBURY
Incomplete rectangular enclosures, parallel
lines and linear features. Features extend
a short distance into square 9973 (not
plotted).
ST JOSEPH 57 VF 91.

9974 SU 97 SE Area centred SU 992747
OLD WINDSOR
Double concentric circle cut across by parallel
lines and linear feature.
ST JOSEPH 57 VF 76, 81.
Excavations from 1953 to 1958 at Kingsbury,
the presumed site of Edward the Confessor's
Palace (SU 991745), by the Berkshire
Archaeological Society and Hope-Taylor
revealed Saxon and Norman occupation
from the seventh to the twelfth centuries
AD, including the sites of two water mills.
Only a preliminary report has ever been
published (see WILSON & HURST 1958),

9875 9975 SU 97 NE Area centred SU
992753
OLD WINDSOR
Incomplete rectangular enclosure with
entrances on S and W sides. Irregular
oval enclosure with two possible entrances
on E side. Linear features and scattered
pits.
ST JOSEPH 57 VF 82, 89.

9975 SU 97 NE Area centred SU 994759
DATCHET
Rectangular enclosure crossed by linear
feature.
ST JOSEPH 57 VF 87.

9976 SU 97 NE Area centred SU 992762
DATCHET *Pl. 14*
Complex of features including 4 circles,
subrectangular enclosure with entrance on
E side, pit alignment and series of elongated
rectangular enclosures arranged in parallel with
N-S orientation. Small rectangular enclosure.
Parallel lines, linear features and scattered pits.
ST JOSEPH 56 TH 82, 84; 57 VF 83-85, 88.

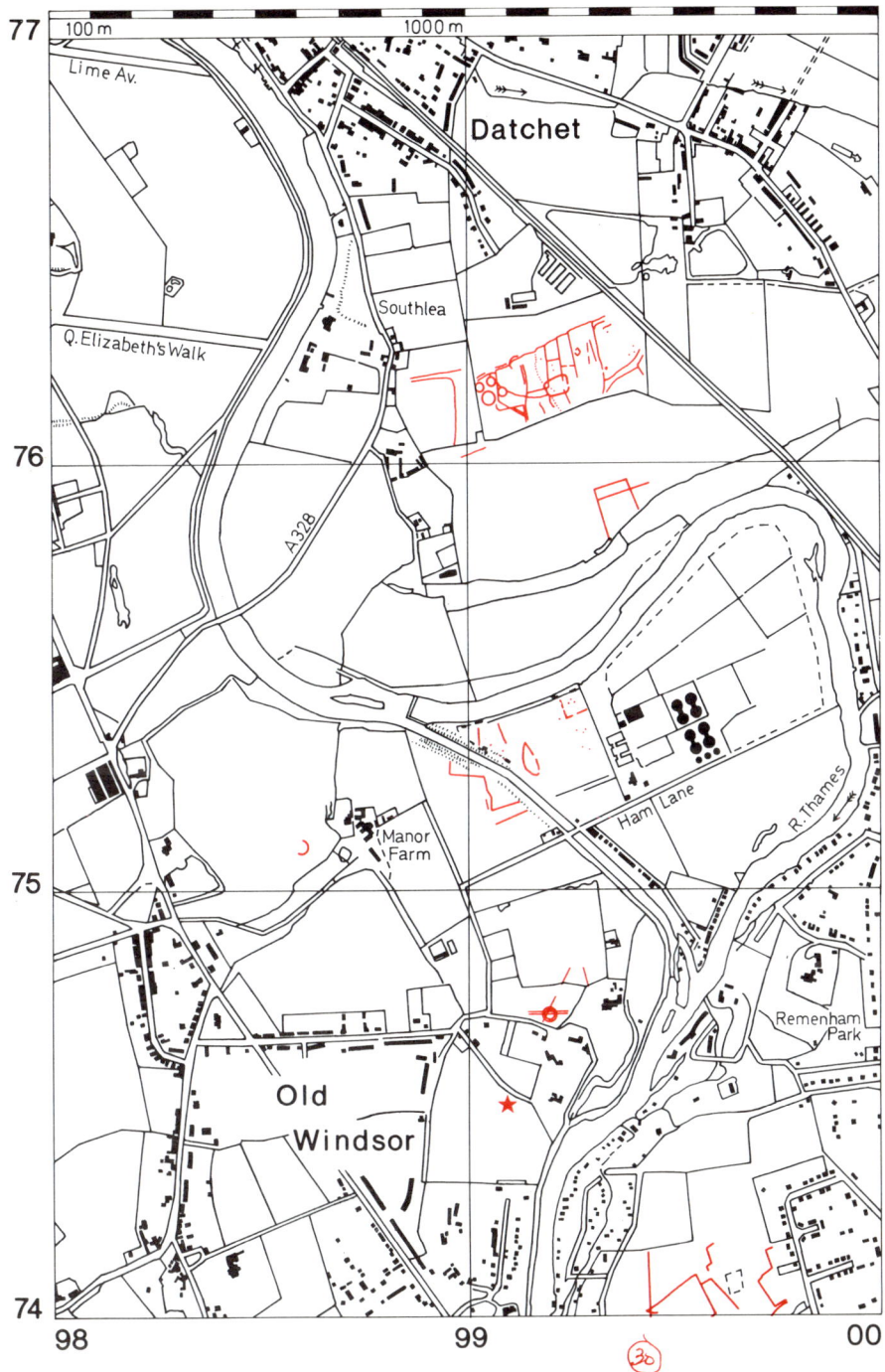

Map 30. Cropmarks around Datchet and Old Windsor

50

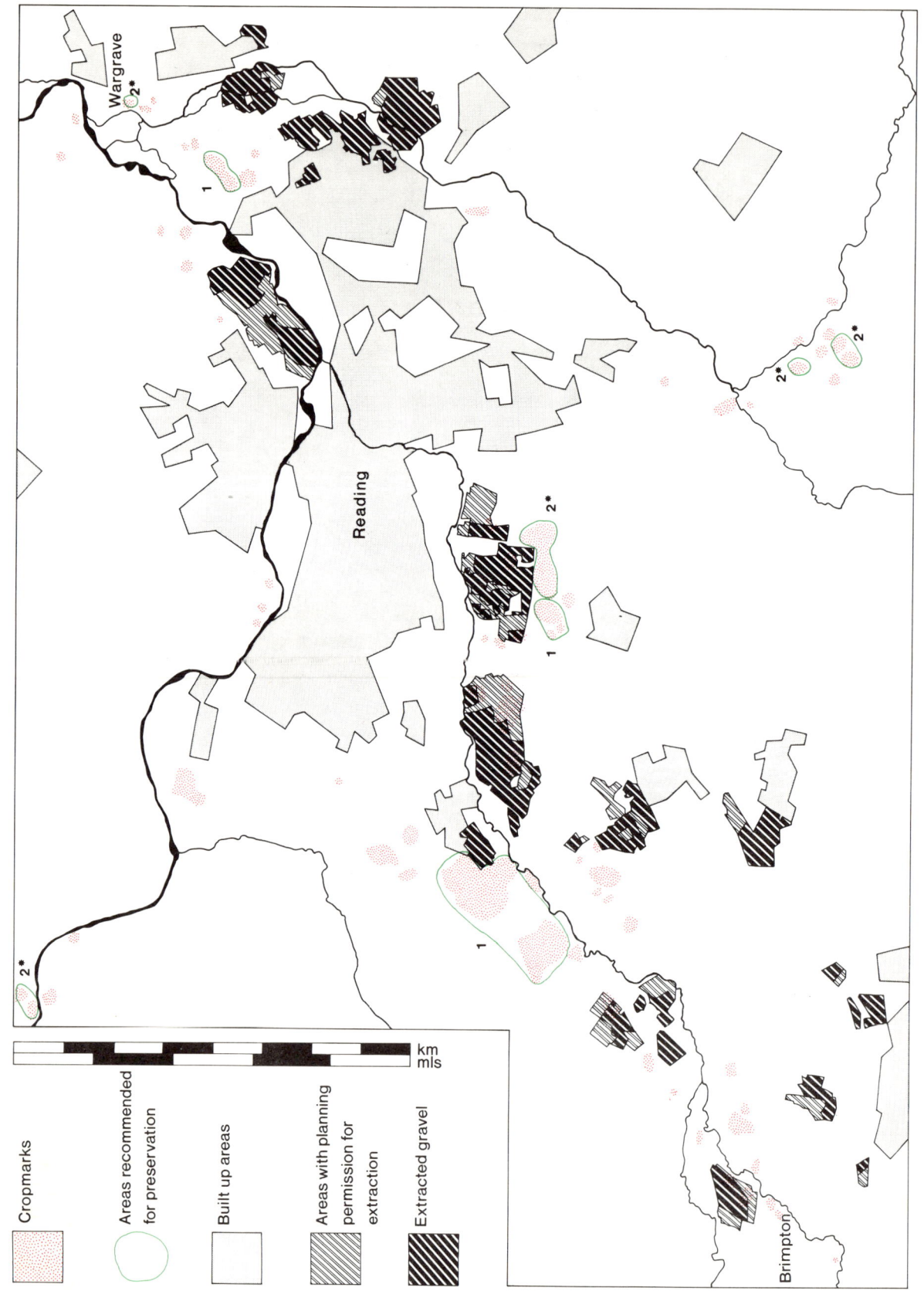

Fig. 8 Developments affecting cropmarks and sites recommended for preservation. Section 1 Thames Valley Goring-Shiplake, and lower Kennet, Loddon, Blackwater valleys

Wargrave

Reading

Brimpton

km
mls

Cropmarks

Areas recommended
for preservation

Built up areas

Areas with planning
permission for
extraction

Extracted gravel

6. DEVELOPMENT FACTORS AFFECTING ARCHAEOLOGICAL SITES

Gravel Extraction

6.1   More archaeological sites in the Thames valley are destroyed by gravel quarrying than by any other agency. In a fast working pit up to 20 acres of land a year disappear into the dragline bucket. In the process any archaeological features are totally and irreversibly lost as whole gravel seams are removed to depths of up to six metres. On the extensive terraces between Greater London and Lechlade in Gloucestershire there are currently over 30 working pits, many of which are affecting areas of proven archaeological importance. Unless an archaeological campaign is organised on a comparable scale then little meaningful evidence can be salvaged.

6.2   On a national scale the consumption of aggregates of all kinds in Britain has risen from an estimated 62 million tonnes in 1948 to 240 million tonnes in 1972—an increase of 400%. Increasing demand from the construction industry is expected to push this figure up to 330 million tonnes by 1980. The resources available for rescue archaeology must be substantially increased if the continuing increase in the demand for aggregates is not to result in the destruction of irreplaceable archaeological information on an even more massive scale than at present.

6.3   The total production of sand and gravel in 1972 was a record 117 million tonnes of which only 12 million tonnes were dredged from the sea. The remaining 105 million tonnes were won at the expense of the historic landscape. In 1972 the Middle and Upper Thames gravel region produced 11·5 million tonnes of gravel or about 10% of the national total. This is the equivalent of 276 hectares (615 acres) of land, of which the greater proportion was located on the terraces of the Thames and its tributaries, which can be shown to have been densely occupied for the past 5000 years.

6.4   Within the Middle and Upper Thames gravel region there are 2700 square miles of gravel-bearing deposits, of which approximately 24,000 hectares are thought to be free from planning constraints and therefore potentially available for quarrying. As supplies of high quality aggregate close to expanding urban centres diminish, and the demand from the construction industry increases, there will be greater pressure for these resources to be released for development. It is estimated that in the 15 years between 1972 and 1987 the demand for gravel within the region will reach 270 million tonnes or well over twice the present annual production in the country as a whole. To meet this demand 4330 hectares of land will require planning permission for quarrying over and above the 2237 hectares of unworked land for which consent has already been given. Because working pits have to be replaced before they run out it is likely that the majority of this land will receive planning permission before 1980. Whilst it is to be hoped that increased imports of crushed rock and marine-dredged gravel may reduce this figure slightly, there can be little doubt that the greater part will be quarried within the region itself. Failure to make special provision for the protection of important cropmarked areas during the planning process will inevitably lead to the loss of some of the country's most extensive archaeological sites.

6.5   The pressure on gravel resources in the Thames valley as a whole is relatively high because of the local rate of suburban expansion and the proximity of London, where there is a greater demand for gravel than can be met by the rapidly dwindling resources within the Greater London area. It is clear from *Figs. 8 & 9* that suburban development and gravel extraction have already severely restricted the scope of archaeological analysis in some parts of our area. This is particularly the case where the gravel deposits are most extensive in the lower reaches of the Kennet valley southwest of Reading and in the Thames valley to the south and east of Slough.

6.6   In 1972 the government appointed an Advisory Committee on aggregates under the chairmanship of Mr Ralph Verney. In a preliminary report, completed in September 1973, it recommended that increased effort should be devoted to encouraging the use of lower grade aggregate such as colliery waste, blast furnace slag and pulverised fuel ash. Whilst it is hoped that this recommendation will eventually lead to the development of alternative sources of aggregates it is unlikely to alter the demand for gravel in the foreseeable future.

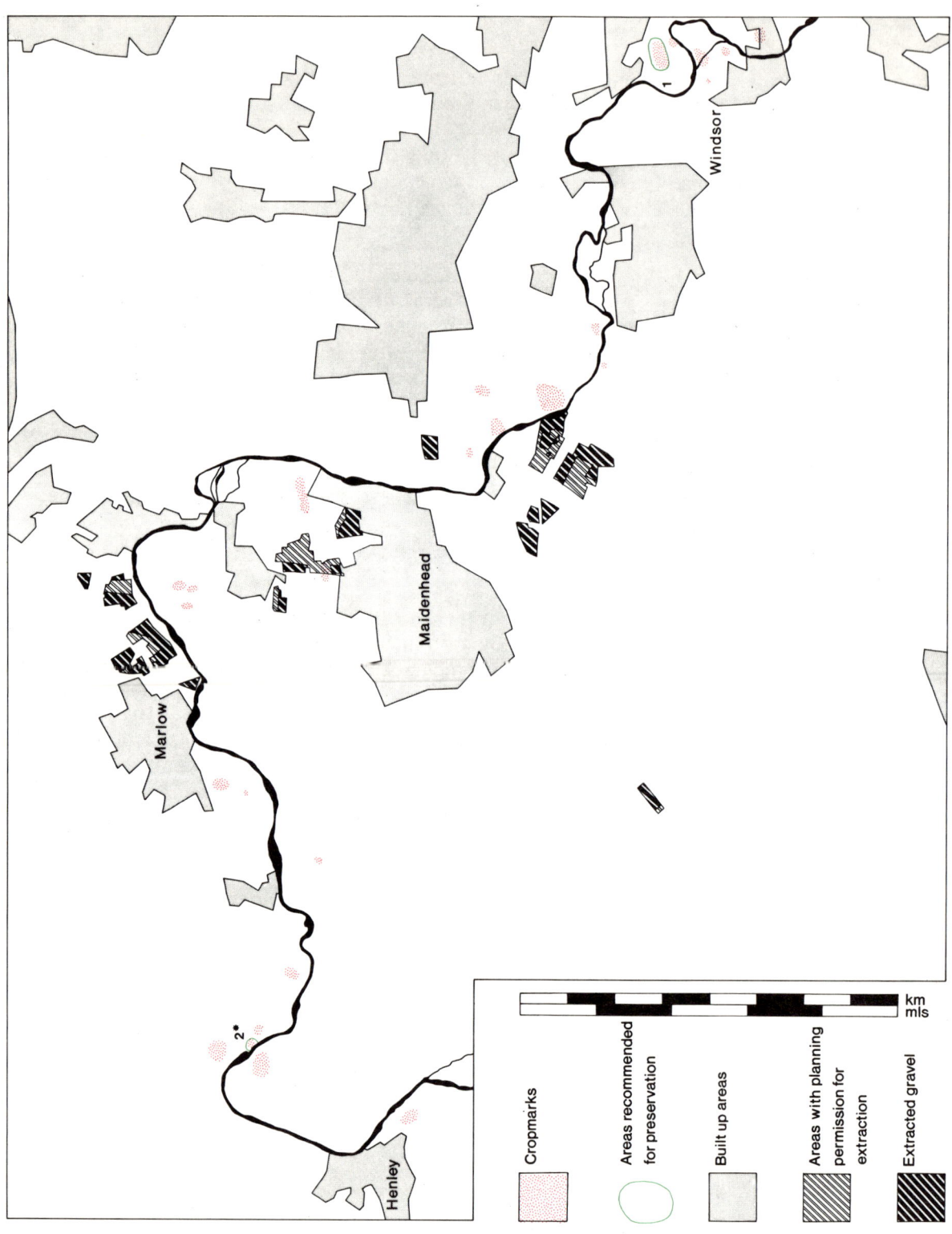

Fig. 9 Developments affecting cropmarks and sites recommended for preservation. Section 2 Thames Valley
Shiplake-Wraysbury

6.7   It is the intention of the Berkshire and Oxfordshire planning authorities to confine gravel extraction whenever possible within areas that already support working pits *(Final report of the working party on sand and gravel; Middle and Upper Thames gravel region).* Such a policy would result in increased pressure on the remaining cropmarked complexes in the lower Kennet valley around Pingewood *(Map 11)* and Aldermaston *(Map 1),* and in the Thames Valley near Bray *(Map 28).* Although any further destruction of sites in these areas can only be deplored there are reasons for preferring a policy of concentrated working to continued piecemeal development. In parts of the lower Kennet valley, for example, widespread working has resulted in the partial destruction and dissection of integrated cropmarked complexes to the point where the archaeological potential of the area has been seriously diminished. Continued development in this area would be more acceptable in the long term than an extension of the damage into the few remaining parts of the region that are still free from development. The limited archaeological resources could then be concentrated in restricted areas of working provided that the long term preservation of unaffected areas, such as the Loddon-Blackwater valley south of the M4 *(Maps 12, 14 & 15; Fig. 8),* and the Ufton Nervet-Englefield area *(Maps 7 & 8)* could be assured. The only notable exception to this policy would be in the case of the cropmarks around Pingewood *(Map 11 squares 6869 & 6969)* which still offer opportunities for the study of substantial remains of probable Iron Age & Romano-British date.

Suburban Exapnsion

6.8   Considerable areas of the Middle Thames gravels have already been built over and the suburban areas will continue to grow in response to the rapidly increasing local population. It is difficult to assess the impact of suburban spread around the larger towns such as Reading, Maidenhead and Slough because information on the distribution of sites is lacking in the immediately surrounding areas. Neither is it possible to make a reliable estimate of the number of sites affected in the past except by inference from the large numbers of stray finds of all periods that have been recovered from within built up areas.

6.9   Although buildings with only shallow foundations may destroy only the superficial features of an archaeological site the effects of urban expansion are nevertheless deleterious. Deep trenches for pipes and cables dissect integrated sites into fragments. The working conditions on building sites generally prohibit worthwhile investigation once construction has begun. Salvage programmes must therefore concentrate on the discovery and excavation of archaeological sites beforehand. Intensive ground and air surveys are essential well in advance of building schemes. At present fieldwork is taking place on the southeast side of Reading between Earley and the M4, where an area of 278 acres has been scheduled for housing. Only one site is at present known to be affected *(Map 13)* although others probably remain to be discovered.

Roads

6.10   The destruction of archaeological sites that has accompanied the growth of the motorway network has attracted considerable attention (FOWLER 1971). The unexpectedly large number of previously unknown sites that were discovered during these operations serves to emphasise the continuing need for intensive fieldwork in areas scheduled for development. Although there are currently no major road schemes in the region which are likely to affect known sites this was not the case when the M4 was built in 1969-70. At that time a limited salvage operation was conducted but only two sites were excavated in advance—a pair of ring-ditches near Burghfield and a Roman villa at Maidenhatch in Berkshire. Serious damage was however inflicted on two large cropmarked complexes; at Dorney Reach in Buckinghamshire, and near Pingewood, south of Reading in Berkshire *(Maps 11 and 28 and Plates 7 and 8),* neither of which was investigated before or during destruction in spite of the fact that both sites had been photographed from the air up to ten years beforehand.

Agriculture

6.11   Most of the agricultural land on the Middle Thames gravels is given over to arable farming apart from low-lying fields near the rivers which are under permanent pasture. Whilst, in general, farming practices interfere very little with archaeological sites, there are cases where ploughing has a deleterious effect. Where the soil is thin, ploughing causes the erosion of the underlying subsoil surface with the consequent destruction of fragile features such as floor levels and post holes. At the Roman villa at Hambleden in Buckinghamshire

(Map 21) all the tesellated floors had been destroyed by ploughing although the wall footings were in a better state of preservation. Surface scatters of pottery and building rubble on ploughed fields attest to the disturbance of archaeological deposits. In most cases the damage is not serious as marling of the light soils is unnecessary and ploughing does not usually occur to great depths. Nevertheless a survey of the extent of plough damage is urgently needed on sites where erosion is evidently taking place. In some instances where a site has only recently come under plough it may be appropriate to make acknowledgement payments under the Field Monuments Act as an inducement to return the site to permanent pasture.

Forestry

6.12 Forestry plantations and woodlands adversely affect archaeological sites because the tree roots disturb stratified deposits and prise apart buried stonework. Dense tree cover also hampers ground fieldwork and prevents survey from the air. Areas of land scheduled for afforestation should therefore be surveyed in advance and existing plantations examined for evidence of earthworks. There is a particular need for a survey of the forestry plantations on the south side of the Kennet valley where there are also extensive gravel quarries.

Treasure Hunting

6.13 Although this is not at present a serious problem in the Middle Thames region the continuing availability of cheap metal detectors puts many archaeological sites at risk. In some parts of the country the irresponsible, and often illegal, depredation of sites has become a major threat. All unwarranted digging on archaeological sites is to be discouraged and landowners are urged to protect sites in their care.

7. ARCHAEOLOGICAL PROVISION

7.1 There has been less archaeological activity in this region than in the Upper Thames. Although there have been sporadic excavations on both threatened and unthreatened sites the most serious lack has been in organised fieldwork and ground survey. As a result of this omission no clear policies towards gravel sites have been formulated and there has sometimes been confusion between archaeological interests on the one hand and planners and commercial developers on the other.

Berkshire and Oxfordshire Archaeological Committees and Units

7.2 The Berkshire Archaeological Committee was formed in 1973 in response to the growing awareness of the pressures to which the archaeological landscape is being subjected. A wide range of opinion is represented on the Committee which includes representatives of the County Council, District Councils and the Ancient Monuments Inspectorate in addition to local archaeologists. At present this Committee is the only body receiving government funds for rescue archaeology in Berkshire. In the financial year 1974-5 the total budget for rescue archaeology in the county was £10,000 which was used to commission surveys of the archaeological implications of road, suburban and gravel developments and to carry out a limited number of salvage excavations. It is hoped that in the near future these activities will be expanded to cover a survey of plough damage on the chalklands of the Berkshire Downs. In April 1975 the Berkshire Archaeological Unit was formally established as the means of effecting all rescue work in the new county of Berkshire.

7.3 The gravel terraces of the north bank of the Thames lie partly in south Oxfordshire and partly in Buckinghamshire. The south Oxfordshire section is well catered for by the Oxfordshire Archaeological Unit whose work has already been described in the Upper Thames survey (BENSON & MILES 1975) and will not be enlarged on here. At present the responsibility for rescue archaeology in Buckinghamshire lies with the County Museum in Aylesbury.

Local Authorities

7.4   The Berkshire County and District Councils are represented on the Berkshire Archaeological Committee. Although the Berkshire County Council contributed £2000 towards the cost of rescue excavations in Abingdon in 1973 the work of the Berkshire Archaeological Unit is not at present supported by local authority funds. The Reading Museum is supported by the Reading Borough Council and its officers have been engaged in work on the gravels at various times in the past.

Local Museums

7.5   Collections of finds from the gravels are stored and displayed in the Reading Museum as well as an important collection of material dredged from the Thames which is on loan from the Thames Water Authority. The Museum also maintains records of many sites in the area and has in the past sponsored a small number of rescue and research excavations on gravel sites. More recently its equipment has been made available for use by the Berkshire Archaeological Unit. Finds from the Kennet valley gravels can be seen in the Newbury Museum which also keeps records of local sites.

University of Reading

7.6   Reading University incorporates a Department of History in which archaeology is taught to first degree level. On occasion the staff of the department have conducted training excavations, some of which were on gravel sites. Although the role of students in rescue work is necessarily limited by academic commitments, it is hoped that they may contribute towards the activities of the unit. There are also valuable library facilities within the university.

Conservation

7.7   Facilities for conservation are strictly limited. There is a well equipped conservation laboratory within the Reading Museum but there is only one trained technician whose primary commitment is to museum material. Whilst these facilities have been made available to the unit they are likely to be inadequate for handling large quantities of material and it may therefore be necessary to establish a basic laboratory within the unit itself to carry out urgent conservation work.

Local Societies

7.8   The Berkshire Archaeological Society is the longest standing and best established society in the region. In past years it has sponsored excavations on gravels sites and the membership includes a number of experienced part-time excavators. More recently it has concentrated on fieldwork and has undertaken a study of earthworks on the chalklands, and pioneered the plotting of aerial photographs before the present survey was initiated. The society also publishes an annual journal — the Berkshire Archaeological Journal — which contains excavation reports, short articles and records of finds reported to the Reading Museum. The Newbury and District Field Club has a long record of fieldwork and publication. There are also two small societies in Maidenhead. Like the Upper Thames, the Middle Thames falls within the region served by the Council for British Archaeology Group 9 which covers Bedfordshire, Berkshire, Buckinghamshire, Northamptonshire and Oxfordshire. This publishes an annual newsletter containing summaries of recent excavations, arranges conferences on topics of local interest and acts as a valuable forum for discussion.

Kennet Valley Research Committee

7.9   This committee is carrying out a study of the geologically recent sediments of the Kennet valley with a particular view towards locating Mesolithic occupation sites similar to the one excavated at Thatcham. The lower Kennet valley offers good opportunities for recovering well preserved archaeological material in the thick and widely distributed deposits of waterlogged alluvium and peat. It is hoped that research into their history will throw light on the local development of settlement and land use. There are particularly good opportunities here for pollen analysis which could fill an important gap in our knowledge (cf. CHURCHILL 1962). F.R. Froom has made a valuable contribution to the study of Mesolithic settlement in the Kennet Valley by his high standard of fieldwork and excavation.

Commercial Firms

7.10   No campaign of rescue archaeology on the gravels can hope to be successful without the active support of the gravel operators themselves. It is therefore gratifying to record that the companies are becoming increasingly aware of the irreversible damage that their operations are doing to the archaeological landscape. It is hoped that they will contribute generously towards offsetting the cost of this damage by financially supporting the work of the unit.

National Organisations

7.11   Several national organisations are actively supporting archaeological work in the Middle Thames area:

(a) The Directorate of Ancient Monuments and Historic Buildings. Funds are provided by the Department of the Environment for rescue work which are administered through this body, whose staff are also responsible for the administration of the Ancient Monuments Acts.

(b) The Royal Commission on Historical Monuments. In 1960 this Commission was responsible for the publication of *A Matter of Time,* which was the first major attempt to draw attention to the rate at which sites were being destroyed by gravel quarrying. The Air Photograph Unit continues to play an essential role in taking aerial photographs of sites over the whole country and in building up a national archive of photographs from all sources. Many of the prints used to compile this survey came from this collection.

(c) The Ordnance Survey (Archaeological Division) maintains a nationwide archive of archaeological records derived from a variety of sources. These records were extensively consulted during the compilation of the gazetteer.

8. ARCHAEOLOGICAL PROBLEMS AND POTENTIAL

8.1   More than forty years of aerial survey have conclusively demonstrated that ancient settlements and monuments are widely distributed over the landscape, including areas which were until recently thought to have been sparseley populated. Large scale development projects such as motorway building, which involve the wholesale removal of topsoil, have brought to light many sites whose presence was previously unsuspected. The rapidly increasing body of archaeological data must necessarily lead us to a selective approach to excavation. Not all sites offer the same possibilities of providing information which is relevant in solving current problems. The need to adopt a selective approach is even more important in the context of rescue archaeology since sites are being destroyed faster than they can be investigated, given our limited resources of labour and money. Rescue archaeology can only be expected to yield worthwhile results if it operates within the context of specific policies designed to answer regional problems. Recent assessments of the role of rescue archaeology have stressed the need for intensive regional surveys of the distribution of sites as a prerequisite for the design of appropriate rescue programmes (eg. RENFREW 1973). It is intended that this survey shall be used in conjunction with surveys of the Upper Thames gravels (BENSON & MILES 1974 for Oxfordshire; under preparation for Gloucestershire) to introduce a coherent policy of rescue work to cover the Thames gravels above London.

8.2   The archaeological potential of the Middle Thames region is limited by the extent to which the area has already been built over and affected by gravel pits (see *Figs. 8 & 9).* 18% of the land surface area shown in *Figure 8* and 13% of that in *Figure 9* has been covered by dense housing or destroyed by gravel quarrying. If villages, roads and woodlands are taken into account the figure would approach 20 or 25%. Compared with the Oxfordshire gravels the Middle Thames terraces are less extensive. This may explain the smaller number of large cropmarked complexes, which appear to be restricted to the lower Kennet valley *(Maps 7, 8 & 11)* and the Loddon and Blackwater valleys *(Maps 14 & 15);* elsewhere the known cropmarked sites are smaller and more scattered. Although this difference might be explained as the result of a different pattern of settlement development it may equally well be a distorted picture resulting from the comparative lack of aerial survey.

8.3   The range of recognisable cropmark types is broadly similar to that displayed on the Upper Thames gravels. Identifiable settlements of the second and third millenium BC (Neolithic and Bronze Age) are wholly lacking, and for these periods the record is restricted to funerary and supposedly ceremonial monuments. It may be that such early settlements were not sufficiently substantial to have left remains that can be located from the air. Alternatively the effects of erosion on slopes and high ground, coupled with deposition in the valley floors, may have destroyed or buried them under deposits of silt. Geological dating of the superficial silt may help to throw light on this problem.

8.4   Some more substantial structures do however survive. At Sonning there is an example of a cursus with a rectangular terminal pierced by a causeway (*Map 19 7675* and *Plate 11*) which may be dated by comparison with excavated examples to the middle or late third millenium BC. There may be a second example near Goring *(Map 6 6079)*, associated with multiple ring-ditches, which would bring the total number of such monuments to around eight in the Thames Valley between London and Lechlade. Apart from the causeway camp near Staines (ROBERTSON-MACKAY 1962), which has now been destroyed, there are no examples of this type of site in the region although there are perhaps three on the upper Thames gravels.

8.5   No large henge monuments of the type found at Dorchester and Stanton Harcourt in Oxfordshire have been identified below Goring, though it is probable that at least some of the large circles, often thought to represent ploughed-out Bronze Age barrows, are structurally related to the henges. Certainly some can be shown to be of late Neolithic date (for example at Englefield: *Map 8 6169 & Plate 3*). This was before burial under round barrows became prevalent. In other cases a domestic function cannot altogether be discounted (CASE 1963; PRYOR 1975). The ambiguities in the evidence recovered from these so called 'ring-ditches' usually forbid a positive identification of their original function. Careful excavation of well preserved examples, avoiding the use of machinery for topsoil stripping, may yet provide more information on this point. There are many examples of ring-ditches in our area occuring either singly, in clusters (eg. *Map 6 6079; & Map 16 7576)* or linear arrangements (*Map 8 6169 & Plate 3)*.

8.6   It is not until the latter part of the first millenium BC (the Iron Age) that we can identify settlements with any degree of certainty. These consist of enclosures of various shapes which sometimes contain faint hut circles and are often associated with trackways, and pits that were used for grain storage and rubbish disposal. Only one example of such a site has been even partially excavated in this region north east of Ufton Nervet (*Map 8 6168 & 6169 & Plate 4)*. It consisted of a subrectangular enclosure with a wide trackway leading up to it from the south and contained a number of pits and post holes but no hut emplacements (MANNING *BAJ* – in press). The enclosure went out of use in about 25 AD and was superseded by a more regular Romano-British enclosure system. There are many other settlements which can probably be dated to the first millenium, (eg *Map 11 6969 & Plate 7; Map 15 7264, 7363 & Plate 9; Map 19 7776; & Map 30 9976)*. Although individual elements of many such settlements have been excavated in the Upper Thames region only one complete site plan has been recovered.

8.7   The study of Romano-British settlement in the area has been dominated by interest in the nearby cantonal capital of Calleva Atrebatum, at Silchester in Hampshire. Villas have been excavated at Maidenhatch, and Cox Green near Maidenhead, in Berkshire, and at Hambleden in Buckinghamshire. There is a further villa site at Mill End, Buckinghamshire *(Map 21 7884)* and possible ones at Ufton Nervet *(Map 8 6269)* and Basildon *(Map 6 6079)* in Berkshire. Little attention has been paid to farmsteads or enclosure systems except for the excavations at Ufton Nervet, where a single enclosure of this period was partially investigated. There is scope for more extensive work on other similar sites, for example around Swallowfield *(Map 15 & Plate 9)*, where there are settlements of probable Romano-British date spread over a wide area, possibly overlying earlier, Iron Age, enclosures.

8.8   Apart from excavations on the supposed site of Edward the Confessor's palace at Old Windsor *(Map 30 9974)* there has been no work on sites of Saxon date in this area. Settlements do undoubtedly exist and their apparent absence is most likely due to inexperience in identifying Grubenhäuser, or small sunken hut floors, that are characteristic of the period. A single hut of this type was examined during the Ufton Nervet excavations and fragments of a Saxon cemetery were found during railway construction north of Maidenhead in 1854 *(Map 26 8885)*.

8.9 Although there are sites of two deserted mediaeval villages in the area *(Maps 9 & 10* & BERESFORD & HURST 1962) neither has been located on aerial photographs, and features of this period are largely confined to occasional traces of ploughed-out ridge and furrow systems. West of Theale *(Map 7 6270* & *6370)* there is an unusual series of elongated rectangular enclosures which coincide in part with the present Theale-Englefield parish boundary and may therefore represent an extensive medieval field boundary system.

8.10 No samples of animal bones or seeds have been examined from archaeological contexts. Similarly studies of ditch sediments, soil profiles, and land snail faunas have been neglected so that information on past economic strategies and environmental conditions is wholly lacking. Pollen analyses were undertaken at the time of the excavations on the Mesolithic site at Thatcham (WYMER 1962) but in general much more work of this kind needs to be done. Further advantage should be taken of the thick waterlogged sediments that exist in the Kennet valley for more extensive work on pollen.

———————— O ————————

9. PRESERVATION, SURVEY AND EXCAVATION

9.1 The limited financial and organisational resources that are available for rescue work dictate a selective archaeological policy in which a balance must be achieved between preservation and excavation.

Preservation

9.2 Preservation has an important role to play in archaeological policy for two reasons. In the first place continuing advances in the techniques of excavation and sampling, such as we have seen over the last thirty years, will detract from the value of excavations undertaken now. Secondly our conceptual models of the past are changing rapidly and generating interest in a wider range of problems. Excavations designed to solve current problems may well fail to provide information that could be retrieved by different methods at a later date.

9.3 It is important that areas of high archaeological value should be taken into account when planning proposals are being considered. Since areas vary in their archaeological importance it has been thought advisable to include a system of grading, similar to that adopted in the Upper Thames gravels survey (BENSON & MILES 1974, para. 11.2, p. 102). The distribution of areas that have already been destroyed and the likelihood of future development have been taken into account as well as purely archaeological factors. (see *Appendix* and *Figs. 8 & 9).).*

> Category 1: Areas which should be preserved. These have been chosen because they offer unusually good opportunities for the study of extensive or complete sites. In most cases they are unlikely to be threatened by development.
>
> Category 2*: Areas where preservation is desirable. If development is proposed then large scale excavation would be essential.
>
> Category 2: Areas with remains of lesser importance than 2* where excavation would be desirable in the event of development. These areas are not marked on *Figs. 8 & 9.*
>
> Category 3: Areas with proposed developments; prior survey and a watching brief should automatically be carried out in these areas. Although some cropmarks may be visible, prior excavation may not be thought advisable. These areas are not marked on *Figs. 8 & 9.*

Survey

9.4   There is an overriding need for systematic survey work throughout the region with particular emphasis on areas where future developments are likely. Continued annual aerial photography must be considered a priority, aiming at a more comprehensive coverage of the gravels and other subsoils, and taking in areas that have previously been neglected. This should be accompanied by accurate and detailed plotting of cropmarks on a large scale, particularly where excavations are planned. An intensive programme of surface fieldwork should also be attempted, to cover the whole region, perhaps initially on a parish basis. The success of this fieldwork operation depends largely on the extent of participation by members of local societies and other volunteers.

Excavation

9.5   A planned programme of excavation should be effected within a broader framework of research priorities. Large scale excavations, spread over several years, should be carried out on complexes which are being progressively destroyed. Preference should be given to sites which have been selected on academic grounds, taking into account the range of sites remaining in the region as a whole.

9.6   Small-scale salvage excavations should be conducted on sites that are less extensive or of only minor importance. Elsewhere watching briefs should be maintained in areas whose archaeological potential is uncertain.

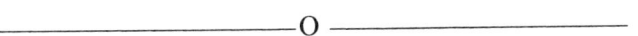

10. RECOMMENDATIONS

Planning

10.1   Provision must be made for the protection and preservation of areas of outstanding archaeological value during the planning process. Particular attention should be paid to areas designated Category 1 and Category 2* in the *Appendix*, and outlined in green in *Figs. 8 & 9*.

10.2   The need for advice on the archaeological implications of projected developments could best be satisfied by the appointment of an archaeological officer within the Berkshire County Planning Department. Such an arrangement is already operating successfully in a number of other counties eg. Essex, Nottinghamshire, Somerset, & Bedfordshire.

10.3   The planning authorities should be encouraged to make use of their powers under the Town and Country Planning Act 1968 to attach conditions to planning consents that would ensure adequate time for the recording of archaeological features in development areas.

Legislation

10.4   The question of legislation in relation to the protection of archaeological sites has not been examined in detail because the subject has already been fully covered in the Upper Thames gravel survey (Benson and Miles 1974, section 9). At the moment no gravel sites in the Middle Thames area are given even the inadequate protection afforded by the Ancient Monuments Acts. Scheduling of important cropmarked complexes, such as those listed in Categories 1 and 2* in the Appendix, should proceed as fast as possible.

Finance

10.5   The budget of the Berkshire Archaeological Unit for 1974-5 was approximately £10,000. This amount had to cover rescue work on sites subject to all kinds of threat including urban expansion and redevelopment, road schemes and gravel extraction. This sum will have to be substantially increased in future if the archaeological response is to be commensurate with the rate of destruction.

10.6   The Berkshire Archaeological Unit is dependent on government funds channelled through the Department of the Environment. If realistic funds are to be made available for rescue archaeology in Berkshire then additional contributions must be sought from local government and commercial firms.

Commercial Firms

10.7   The existing relations with local gravel companies should be extended and operators made aware of the damage to archaeological sites that their work often involves. It is recognised that an effective programme of rescue archaeology on gravels would be impossible without close cooperation and mutual understanding between archaeologists and commercial interests. It is emphasised that it is not the intention of archaeologists to cause unnecessary delay or disruption to gravel operators.

Archaeological Policy

10.8   A comprehensive policy of rescue work on gravel should be designed, taking into account the potential of all gravel deposits in the Thames Valley. To this end prompt discussions will take place between the Berkshire Archaeological Unit, the Oxfordshire Archaeological Unit and the Committee for Rescue Archaeology in Avon, Gloucestershire & Somerset.

10.9   A broad approach to the problems of rescue archaeology should be adopted which takes account of regional priorities and is aimed at a reconstruction of settlement patterns, population densities and economic strategies.

10.10   A selective strategy is suggested for work on gravel sites which makes provision for the long term preservation of areas with outstanding remains. Large scale excavations will be conducted on important sites in development areas supplemented by salvage work and watching briefs elsewhere.

10.11   Particular attention should be paid to the lower Kennet valley where gravel extraction is proceeding fastest.

10.12   An intensive programme of surface fieldwork should be organised in conjunction with local groups and volunteers to investigate areas where development is likely or where known sites are subject to damage or erosion.

10.13   The archaeological records for Berkshire should be organised into a 'sites and monuments record', so as to facilitate the retrieval of information (cf. BENSON 1972).

Air Photography

10.14   There is an urgent need for more comprehensive air survey of the Middle Thames gravels, particularly around Slough and Maidenhead where survey has been limited by the airspace restrictions around Heathrow airport.

Conclusion

10.15   The newly created Berkshire Archaeological Unit will implement a programme of research and rescue archaeology designed to advance our knowledge of the development of settlement in the Middle Thames region. Specific policies for survey, excavation and preservation will be developed in response to problems of both national and regional interest. The success of this programme will be dependent to a large extent on the cooperation and active support of local government and commercial developers who are urged to recognise our collective responsibility to prevent the irretrievable loss of a significant part of our national heritage.

———————————— O ————————————

APPENDIX

SITE GRADING AND PRESERVATION

A suggested grading of cropmarked sites (Figs. 8 and 9)

CATEGORY 1

Sites recommended for preservation

1. Map 7 SU 6270, 6271, 6370, 6371;
   Map 8 SU 6168, 6169, 6269.
   Area southwest of Theale.
   Includes settlement complexes, ring-ditches, probable Roman villa and enclosure system.

2. Map 11 SU 6769, 6869.
   Area northeast of Burghfield.
   Settlement complex and triple-ditched enclosures.

3. Map 19 SU 7675, 7676.
   Area west of Sonning.
   Includes cursus, associated enclosures and ring-ditches.

4. Map 30 SU 9976.
   Area south of Datchet.
   Settlement complex, enclosure system, pit alignment and ring-ditches.

CATEGORY 2*

Preservation desirable. Large-scale excavation essential if any form of development should take place.

1. Map 6 SU 6079, 6080.
   Area south of Goring.
   Barrow cemetery and possible cursus.

2. Map 11 SU 6869, 6969.
   Area northeast of Grazeley.
   Extensive settlement complex. Although damaged by gravel quarrying and the M4 the majority of this site remains intact.

3. Map 17 SU 7877.
   Area southwest of Wargrave.
   Settlement.

4. Map 15 SU 7363.
   Area southeast of Swallowfield.
   Settlement.

5. Map 15 SU 7264.
   Area southeast of Swallowfield.
   Settlement.

6. Map 21 SU 7884.
   Area in Mill End.
   Roman villa.

CATEGORY 2

Excavation essential prior to any development

1. Map 1 SU 5965.
   Area northeast of Aldermaston.
   RB enclosures.

2. Map 19 SU 7776.
   Area northeast of Sonning
   Enclosure.

3. Map 20 SU 7778.
    Area east of Shiplake.
    Enclosures.

4. Map 25 SU 8385, 8485.
    Area southwest of Marlow
    Ring-ditches and associated enclosures.

5. Map 28 SU 9178, 9278.
    Area southwest of Dorney
    Settlement complex and large double concentric circle.

BIBLIOGRAPHY

BENSON, D. 1972 'A sites and monuments record for the Oxford region' *Oxoniensia*, 37, 226-237.

BENSON, D. and D. MILES, 1974 *The Upper Thames Valley: an Archaeological Survey of the River Gravels* (Oxford).

BERESFORD, M.W. & J.G. HURST 1962 'Introduction to a first list of deserted mediaeval village sites in Berkshire' *BAJ*, 60, 92

CASE, H. 1963 'Notes on the finds and on ring-ditches in the Oxford region' *Oxoniensia*, 28, 19-52.

CHURCHILL, D.M. 1962 'The stratigraphy of the Mesolithic sites III and IV at Thatcham, Berkshire, England' *PPS*, 28, 362-37

COCKS, A.H. 1921 'A Romano-British homestead in the Hambleden valley, Bucks' *Archaeologia*, 71, 141-198.

FOWLER, P.J. 1971 'M4 and M5' *Current Archaeology*, 3, 50-51.

HARE, F.K. 1947 'The geomorphology of a part of the Middle Thames' *Proc. Geol. Assoc.*, 58, 294-339.

PIGGOTT, C.M. 1936 'An early settlement at Theale, nr. Reading, Berks' *Trans. Newbury Dist. Field Club*, 7, 146-149.

PIGGOTT, C.M. 1938 'The Iron Age pottery from Theale' *Trans. Newbury Dist. Field Club*, 8, 52-60.

PIGGOTT, C.M. and W.A. SEABY 1937 'An early Iron Age site at Southcote, Reading' *PPS*, 3, 43-57.

PRYOR, F. 1975 'Fengate' *Current Archaeology*, 4, 332-338.

RENFREW, C. 1973 *Social Archaeology: an Inaugural Lecture* (Southampton).

ROBERTSON-MACKAY, R. 1962 'The excavation of the causewayed camp at Staines, Middlesex. Interim report'
    Arch. Newsletter, 7, 131-134.

ROYAL COMMISSION ON HISTORICAL MONUMENTS (ENGLAND) 1960 *A Matter of Time* (London HMSO).

ST JOSEPH, J.K.S. 1966 'Air photography and archaeology' in ST JOSEPH (ed), *The Uses of Air Photography* (Cambridge).

SLADE, C.F. 1964 'A late Neolithic site at Sonning, Berkshire' *BAJ*, 61, 4-19.

SMITH, C.R. 1840 'Roman pavements discovered at Basildon in Berkshire' *Archaeologia*, 40, 447-450.

THOMAS, M.F. 1961 'River terraces and drainage development in the Reading area' *Proc. Geol. Assoc.*, 72, 415-436.

WEBSTER, G. and B. HOBLEY 1964 'Aerial reconnaissance over the Warwickshire Avon' *Arch. Journ.* 121, 1-22.

WILLIAMS, R.G.B. 1973 'Frost and the works of man' *Antiquity*, 47, 19-31.

WILSON, D.M. and J.G. HURST 1958 'Mediaeval Britain in 1957' *Mediaeval Arch.*, 2, 183-185.

WYMER, J. 1962 'Excavations at the Maglemosian sites at Thatcham, Berkshire, England' *PPS*, 28, 329-362.

WYMER, J. 1968 *Lower Palaeolithic Archaeology in Britain as represented by the Thames Valley* (London).

NOTES ON PLATES

Plate 1

The photograph shows an early Iron Age ditch sectioned in the face of a gravel pit at Burcot, near Dorchester-on-Thames. The cereal crop growing above the ditch is visibly darker and taller than that on either side. If viewed from the air the line of the ditch would stand out as a positive cropmark.

Photo: ALLEN 1933   *Ashmolean Museum Copyright*

Plate 2

Rectangular double-ditched enclosure. Almost certainly of Romano-British date.

Map 6 km sq 6178 SU 617778 Basildon
Photo: ST JOSEPH 1959   *Cambridge University Collection: Copyright Reserved*

Plate 3

Row of four conjoined ring-ditches. The smallest ring-ditch (right centre) was excavated in 1963 when Neolithic pottery was found in the ditch filling. The dark coloured area (bottom) represents an abandoned river channel now filled with silt.

Map 7 km sq 6270 SU 624702 Sulhamstead
Photo: CHEETHAM 1974   *Henry Cheetham Copyright*

Plate 4

Settlement area with late Iron Age and Romano-British enclosures (top centre) and a complex of rectangular enclosures of probable Romano-British date (bottom left). The Silchester – Dorchester Roman road crosses the centre of the plate and is linked to the enclosures in the foreground by a branch road.

Map 8 km sq 6169/6269 Ufton Nervet
Photo: ST JOSEPH 1970   *Cambridge University Collection: Copyright Reserved*

Plate 5

Settlement complex area, including central rectangular enclosure, bounded on two sides by trackways. Note that the cropmarks are less well developed in the field with the light-coloured crop at centre left.

Map 11 km sq 6769/6869 Burghfield
Photo: ST JOSEPH 1962   *Cambridge University Collection: Copyright Reserved*

Plate 6

Complex settlement area with enclosures, trackways and pits of probable Iron Age or Romano-British date. The pale scar across the top of the plate is the M4 under construction, with gravel working beyond.

Map 11 km sq 6869 Burghfield
Photo: NMR 1970   *Crown Copyright*

Plate 7

Settlement area with D-shaped and rectangular enclosures, and intersecting trackways. All probably of Iron Age or Romano-British date.

Map 11 km sq 6969 Burghfield
Photo: ST JOSEPH 1969   *Cambridge University Collection: Copyright Reserved*

Plate 8

This photograph covers the same area as plate 7, but one year later. It shows the construction of the M4 across the cropmark complex. Many cropmarked features, including the D-shaped enclosure, were destroyed without investigation.

Map 11 km sq 6969 Burghfield
Photo: ST JOSEPH 1970   *Cambridge University Collection: Copyright Reserved*

Plate 9

Settlement area with two rectangular enclosures and a hut circle. Overlain by ridge and furrow.

Map 15 km sq 7264 Swallowfield
Photo: ST JOSEPH 1970   *Cambridge University Collection: Copyright Reserved*

Plate 10

Small settlement complex (centre) with rectangular enclosures, a hut circle and many pits.

Map 17 km sq 7877 Wargrave
Photo: Fairey Air Surveys 1959   *Reproduced by Courtesy of Reading Museum*

Plate 11   Square ended terminal of a Neolithic cursus pierced by an entrance causeway. In the foreground are two rectangular enclosures and a ring-ditch. Excavation of the small rectangular enclosure in the centre of the photograph showed it to be of Neolithic date and suggests a parallel with the Neolithic/Bronze Age ceremonial complex at Dorchester-on-Thames.

Map 19 km sq 7675 SU 766759 Sonning
Photo: ST JOSEPH 1959   *Cambridge University Collection: Copyright Reserved*

Plate 12   Line of three ring-ditches, including a double concentric example. All probably of late Neolithic or Bronze Age date. Close to the double concentric circle are two irregular enclosures.

Map 25 km sq 8385/8485 SU 838849 Marlow
Photo: ST JOSEPH 1959   *Cambridge University Collection: Copyright Reserved*

Plate 13   Double concentric ring-ditch (Neolithic or Bronze Age) with a rectangular enclosure (top right) of probable Iron Age or Romano-British date.

Map 28 km sq 9178/9278 Dorney
Photo: ST JOSEPH 1957   *Cambridge University Collection: Copyright Reserved*

Plate 14   Settlement area with subrectangular enclosure (top right) associated with a system of parallel, elongated rectangular enclosures (fields?) and a pit alignment. All probably of Iron Age date. Group of four Bronze Age ring-ditches (bottom left).

Map 30 km sq 9976 SU 992762 Datchet
Photo: ST JOSEPH 1957   *Cambridge University Collection: Copyright Reserved*

ERRATA

Page 5 Contents section 10 should read

10.1   Planning
10.4   Legislation
10.5   Finance
10.7   Commercial Firms
10.8   Archaeological Policy
10.14   Air Photography
10.15   Conclusion

Page 54 Section 7.3: For 'BENSON & MILES 1975' read 'BENSON & MILES 1974'.

Page 63 Notes on Plates
Plate 2 map reference should: 'Map 6 km sq 6178 SU 617788 Basildon'.
Plate 12 map reference should read 'Map 25 km sq 8385/8485 SU 840855 Marlow'.

Page 66 Caption for Plate 1 should read 'Cropmark sectioned in a gravel pit at Burcot, near Dorchester'.

66

Plate 1 Cropmark sectioned in a gravel pit at Butcot, near Dorchester

Plate 2 Enclosure near Basildon

Plate 3 Circles near Sulhamstead

Plate 4 Cropmarks near Ufton Nervet

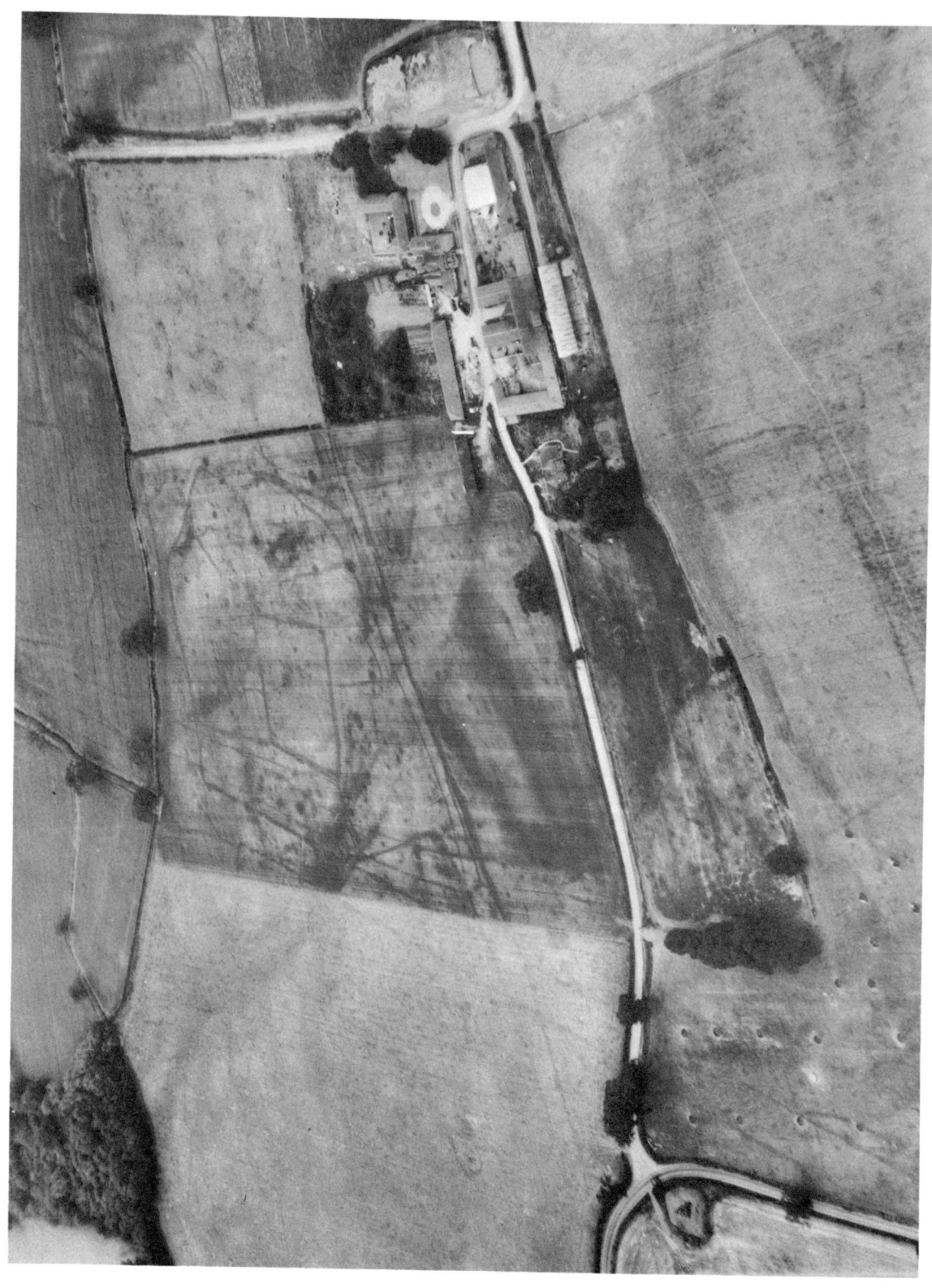

Plate 5 Settlement near Burghfield

Plate 6 Cropmarks near Burghfield

Plate 7 Settlement near Burghfield

Plate 8 Construction of the M4 near Burghfield

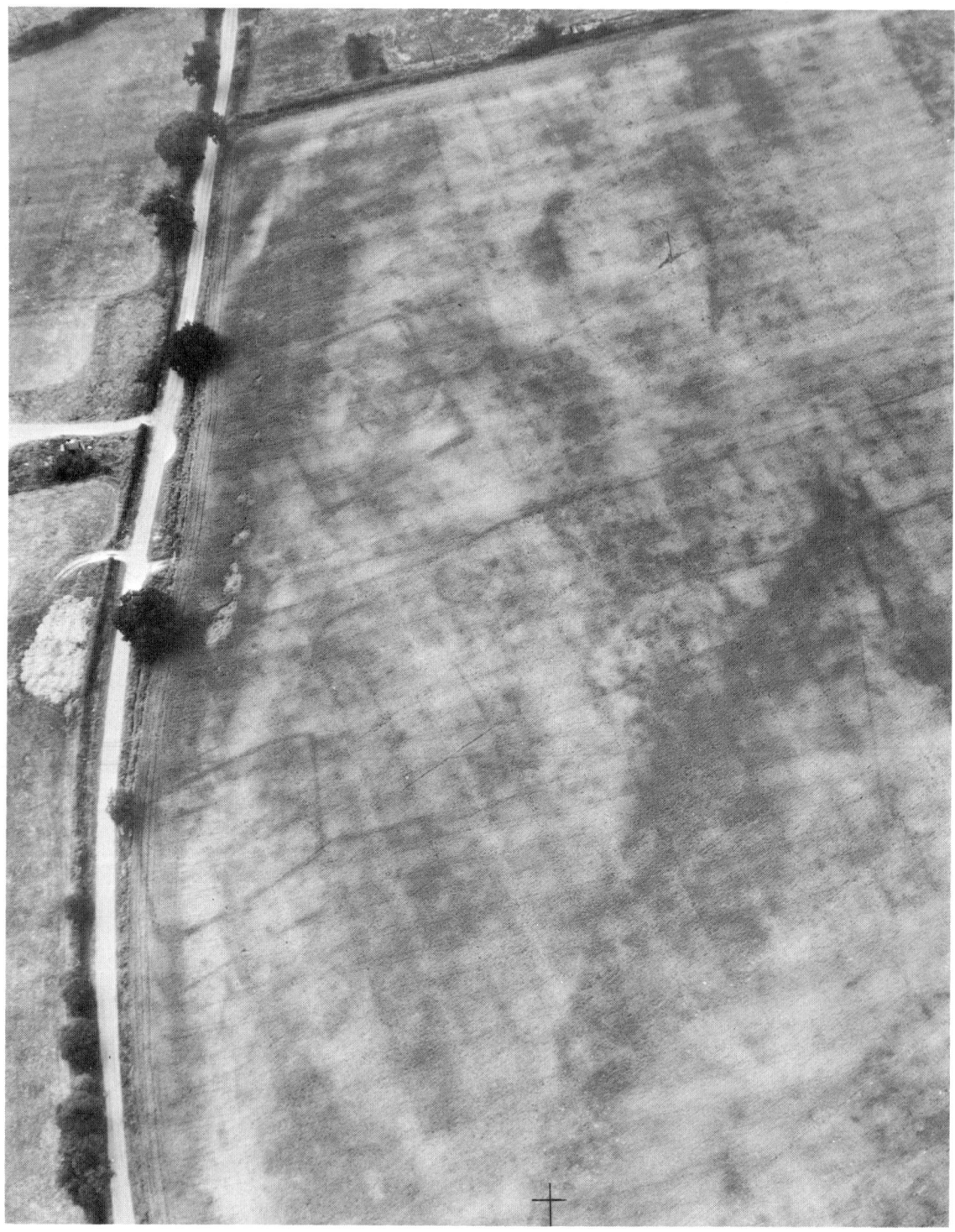

Plate 9   Settlement near Swallowfield

Plate 10 Settlement near Wargrave

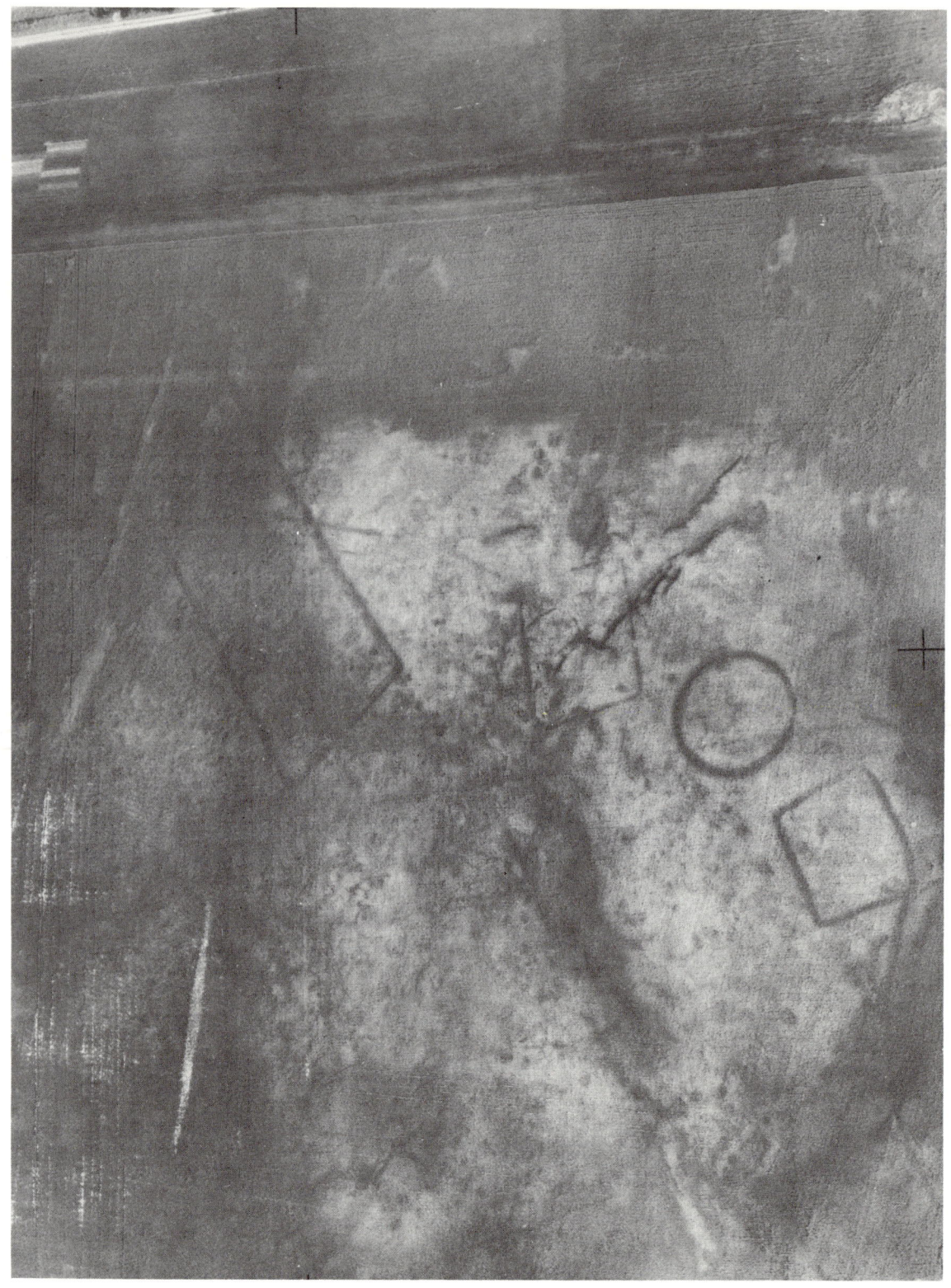

Plate 11 Cropmarks near Sonning

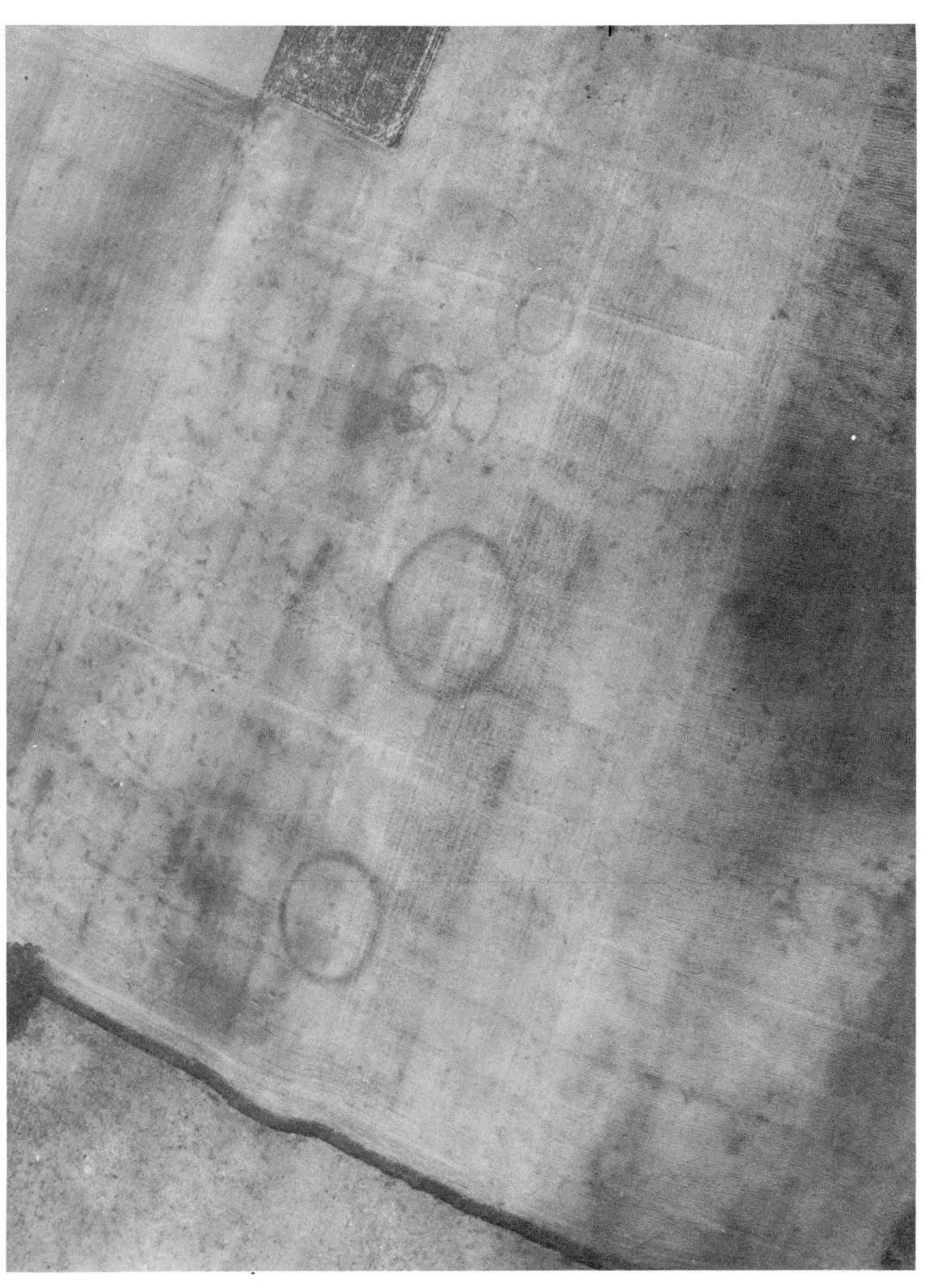

Plate 12 Circles near Marlow

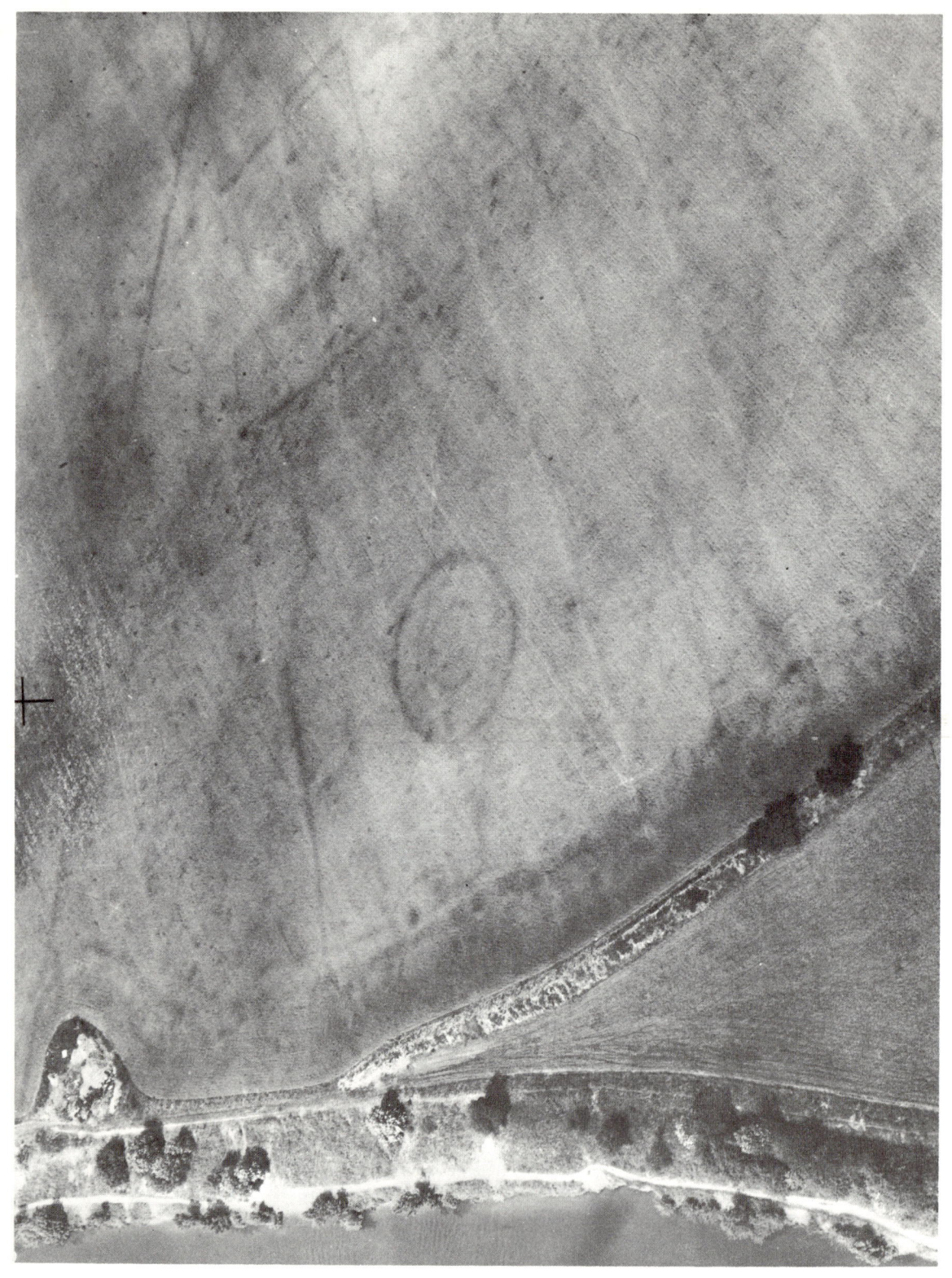

Plate 13 Cropmarks near Dorney

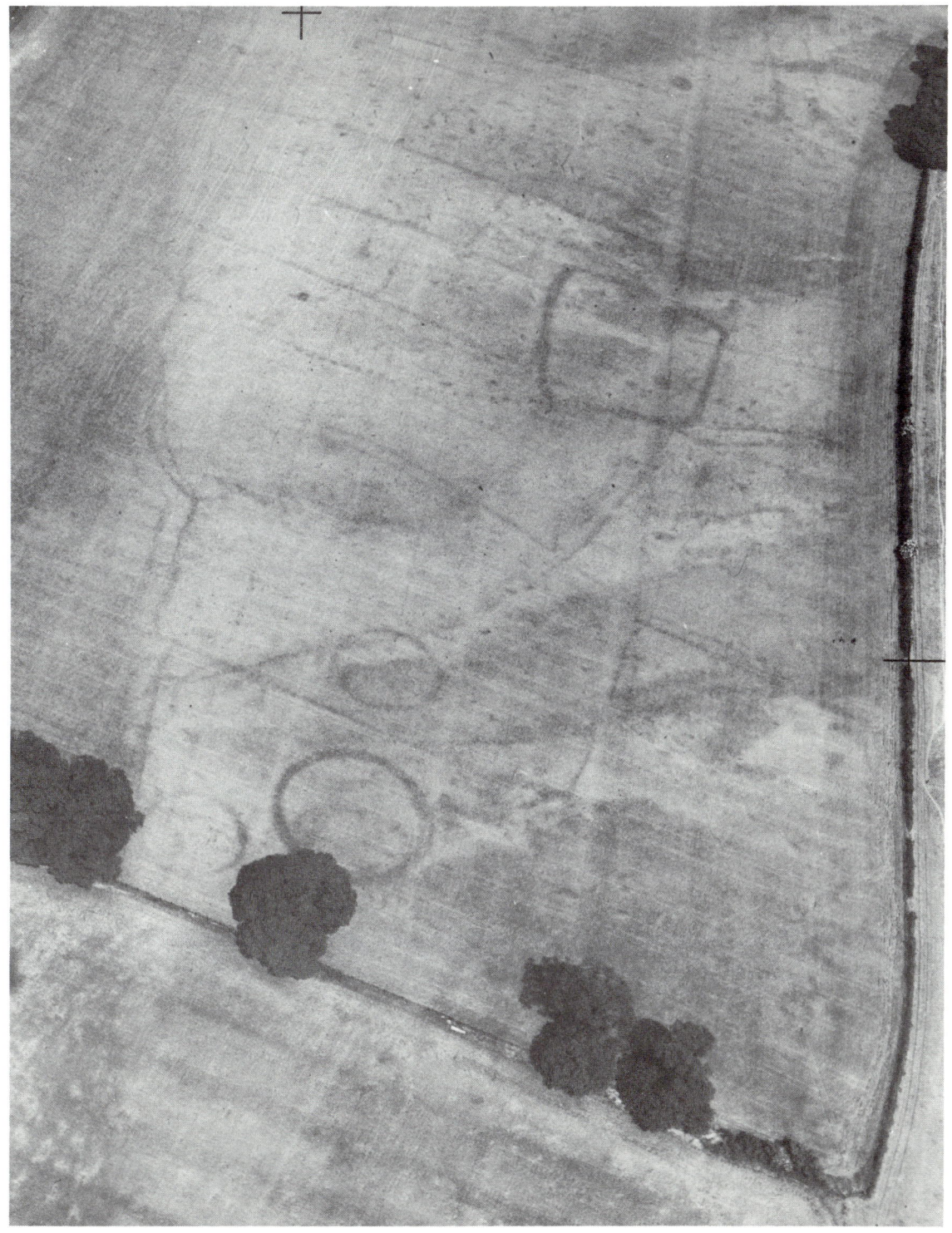

Plate 14 Cropmarks near Datchet